Also by Firoozeh Dumas

Funny in Farsi

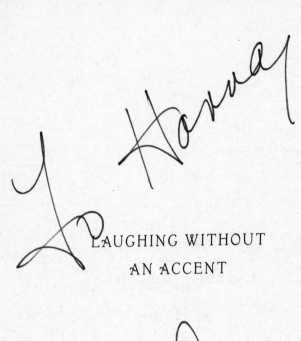

LAUGHING WITHOUT
AN ACCENT

Adventures of

an Iranian American,

at Home

and Abroad

RANDOM HOUSE TRADE PAPERBACKS
NEW YORK

Laughing Without an Accent

FIROOZEH DUMAS

2009 Random House Trade Paperback Edition

Copyright © 2008 by Firoozeh Dumas
Reading group guide copyright © 2009 by Random House, Inc.

Published in the United States by Random House Trade Paperbacks,
an imprint of The Random House Publishing Group,
a division of Random House, Inc., New York.

RANDOM HOUSE TRADE PAPERBACKS and colophon are
trademarks of Random House, Inc.
RANDOM HOUSE READER'S CIRCLE & DESIGN is a registered
trademark of Random House, Inc.

Originally published in hardcover in the United States by Villard Books,
an imprint of The Random House Publishing Group,
a division of Random House, Inc., in 2008.

LIBRARY OF CONGRESS CATALOGING-IN-PUBLICATION DATA

Dumas, Firoozeh.
Laughing without an accent : adventures of an Iranian American,
at home and abroad / Firoozeh Dumas.
p. cm.
ISBN 978-0-345-49957-8 (alk. paper)
1. Dumas, Firoozeh—Anecdotes. 2. Iranian Americans—Biography—Anecdotes.
3. Dumas, Firoozeh—Travel—Anecdotes. 4. Dumas, Firoozeh—Family—Anecdotes.
5. Voyages and travels—Anecdotes. I. Title.
E184.I5D864 2008
910.4—dc22 2008001272

Printed in the United States of America

www.randomhousereaderscircle.com

4 6 8 9 7 5

Book design by Dana Leigh Blanchette

To the Frenchman

CONTENTS

LAUGHING WITHOUT
AN ACCENT

Funny in Persian

Iran does not currently adhere to international copyright laws. This comes as a shock to most people, given Iran's law-abiding image.

Not adhering to international copyright laws means that any book, regardless of origin, can be translated into Persian and sold in Iran. No matter how poorly a book might be translated, the author has no control. No artist wants his name on a work that does not represent him fairly, but in Iran, tell it to the judge, and he doesn't care. When Abbas Milani, a very well respected author and professor, found a Persian translation of his history book, he found it to be completely different from the original. He contacted the publisher in Iran, who told him, "Our translation is better than your book."

Every time a Harry Potter installment is released, there is a mad rush around the world to translate the book. One Iranian publisher divides each book into about twenty sections, giving each section to a different translator. That way, his version, which must resemble a patchwork quilt more than anything J. K. Rowling actually wrote, is the first on the Iranian market.

Knowing such horror stories, I feared the inevitable translation of my memoirs, *Funny in Farsi,* into Persian. *Funny in Farsi* is a collection of humorous vignettes, verbal snapshots of my immigrant family. In that book I was very careful not to cross the line into anything embarrassing or insulting. My goal was to have the subjects of my story laugh with me, not cringe and want to move to Switzerland under assumed names. But for all I knew, a translated version might make my family look like fools. Even though I had not used my maiden name in the original printing of the book, it took about twelve minutes for the average Iranian to figure out my last name, Jazayeri. Iranians are very good that way.

I decided to make my own preemptive strike and find a translator in Iran. This was not as easy as it sounds. Humor, like poetry, is culture-specific and does not always work in translation. What's downright hilarious in one culture may draw blank stares in another.

When we came to America, my family could not figure out why a pie thrown in someone's face was funny. The laugh tracks told us it was supposed to be hilarious, but we thought it was obnoxious. We also saw it as a terrible waste of food, a real no-no for anyone from any country in the world except for the United States.

We were also baffled by Carol Burnett's Tarzan yell. Anyone who watched her show regularly knew that during the audience question-and-answer section, one person would inevitably ask her to do her Tarzan yell. We always hoped she would say, "Not tonight." But instead, she would let out a loud and long yell that left the audience in stitches and us bewildered. "She shouldn't do that," my dad always said. We agreed and waited for all her other sketches, which we loved. There was just something goofy about her that made us laugh, especially when she was with Tim Conway. His humor had much to do with facial expressions and body language, which, thankfully, did not require translation. There is also something universally funny about the contrast between a short man and a tall man, which was played out with Harvey Korman. Given that most of the men in my family are closer in height to Tim Conway than to Harvey Korman, I assume there was among us a nervous understanding of the foibles of the short man.

We also adored Flip Wilson, especially when he became Geraldine. That character sketch, with "Geraldine's" sassy attitude, had us rocking back and forth in laughter on our ugly brown striped sofa. One time, Flip Wilson sang "He put the lime in the coconut" in his high-pitched mock-sultry Geraldine voice, and my father laughed so hard that he cried. I didn't think it was *that* funny, but watching my father laugh made us all laugh. The odd thing is that thirty-five years later, my father *still* remembers some of the words to that song, singing it as Kazem imitating Flip Wilson imitating Geraldine. It sounds nothing like the original, especially when he ekes out a "nee nee nee nee" instead of the forgotten lyrics.

I knew that *Funny in Farsi* would be a difficult book to translate because so much of its humor has to do with the American culture of the seventies. How does one translate "Shake 'n Bake" for cultures where slow cooking, not speed and ease, is the preferred method of food preparation, where a woman standing in her kitchen shaking a drumstick in a plastic bag and looking downright happy would cause concern? How does one convey to someone who has never seen *The Price Is Right* that the words "Come on down!" are always followed by a hysterical person shrieking and jumping up and down?

Through my uncle, who knew someone who knew someone, I was put in touch with a well-known humor translator living in Iran. The same week I started corresponding with him I received a very polite e-mail from Mohammad, another translator in Iran, asking for permission to translate my book. I thanked him but told him I already had someone. I deleted his e-mail.

Before we had a chance to formally agree on anything, my designated translator became ill, and it was obvious that I would have to find someone else. I was stuck, since I had deleted Mohammad's e-mail. A month later, I received another e-mail from Mohammad telling me that he was still interested should I write another book. And this is how Mohammad Soleimani Nia, my translator, came into my life.

To test Mohammad's skill, I asked him to translate one of my stories. I was quite pleased with the results and knew that, serendipitously, I had stumbled upon the right person.

Then we got started. Mohammad translated story by story and e-mailed each one to me. My father and I read each one and I e-mailed back our comments, most of which had to do with nuance. My father particularly objected when Mohammad translated "my father's receding hairline" to "my father's bald head." I immediately sent Mohammad an e-mail quoting my father exactly: "I am not Yul Brynner!" A profusely apologetic e-mail followed.

Some of Mohammad's mistakes revealed what life is like in the Middle East. In one story, I mentioned "eyes meeting across a room and va va va boom." This was translated as "eyes meeting across a room and bombs going off." I had to explain to Mohammad that, in America, "boom" is love.

In a story about Christmas, I wrote about "the bearded fellow" coming down people's chimneys. Mohammad translated this literally. In Iran, however, a "bearded fellow" coming down the chimney is not a happy thought. The idea of going to bed so a bearded man, Khomeini perhaps, can come down the chimney would not cause visions of sugarplums dancing in anyone's head. Instead, one would find frantic people packing their belongings, fast.

The title also had to change. *Funny in Farsi* is not funny in Farsi, or rather Persian, which is the correct name of the language in English. Saying, "I speak Farsi," is like saying, "I speak *français.*" I was more than happy to let that title go since it has been the subject of many long e-mails from Iranians with far too much free time on their hands, accusing me of spreading misinformation about our vastly underappreciated culture. "The language is called Persian!" they tell me. I know. Please, should any reader, Iranian or otherwise, feel the urge to e-mail me with a complaint about the incorrect use of the word "Farsi" in the title of my previous book, please, instead, look up the words "humorous alliteration."

In Iran, the title was changed to *Atre Sombol, Atre Koj,* meaning *The Scent of Hyacinths, the Scent of Pine,* which refers to the contrasting smells of the holidays. The Iranian New Year is associated with the scent of hyacinths, and Christmas, with the scent of pine—not to mention the bearded fellow coming down the chimney, although technically, that should not smell.

Then it was time for the censors. No movie or book can be made in Iran without approval from the government. Although there are no written guidelines stating exactly what is prohibited, common sense dictates that in an Islamic theocracy, nudity, profanity, insulting the religion or government, and perhaps anything having to do with Paris Hilton are all no-nos. Aside from those guidelines, one is at the mercy of the individual government employee assigned to each book. I hoped my stories would end up in the hands of one of those fun-loving, laugh-a-minute censors who would wave his teacup in the air, declaring, "Let's change the name of that street again, this time to Firoozeh Dumas Avenue."

I asked Mohammad how long the government would take to return my book. Surprisingly, there are no guidelines there, either. Perhaps some sort of Oil-for-Guidelines program could be negotiated.

Mohammad told me that the translation for James Joyce's *Ulysses* has been at the censor's office for seventeen years. I imagined the bearded censor sitting as at his desk, book open, chin back, mouth open, snoring loudly. That's an example of a book that could use some nudity.

My stories were returned after six months. Three changes had to be made, two minor, one major.

The censor objected to my describing someone looking as if God had switched her nose with the beak of a toucan. One cannot blame God, I was told. In the Persian version, I reworded the sentence, using a passive voice, claiming that the woman's nose looked as if it had been switched. One would think that in a book of humor some things would be obvious, but apparently not. Perhaps I had written the equivalent of Carol Burnett's Tarzan yell.

I also said that in my next life, I wanted to be Swedish. In Islam, the censor said, there is no next life. There is only one life.

I hope that in my next life, I do not have to deal with censors.

And, sadly, I was forced to remove an entire chapter, "The Ham Amendment." In that chapter, which I considered the soul of my book, I explained my father's philosophy that it does not matter what we eat or whether we are Muslim, Christian, or Jewish; it's how we treat our fellow man that counts. The censor did not agree.

When I told my father about the removal of that particular chapter, he was very upset. He said it was probably because the censor did not believe in shared humanity, at least not with Jews. My father also added that my next book should be entitled, "Accomplishments of Jews I Have Known," interspersed with recipes using ham.

When *Atre Sombol, Atre Koj* was published, it became an instant bestseller. In Iran, if a book sells two thousand copies, it has done well. In the first year of publication, thirty thousand copies were sold. After the second year, sales had reached sixty thousand. Books are passed around in families, so every copy reaches ten people. I have noticed the same trend among Iranians in America. At one book signing early on, an Iranian man asked me to sign my book to "Hassan, Reza, Shirin, Mina, Parvaneh, and Ardeshir." When I asked him how six people were expected to share one book, he laughed. "You're so funny!" he said. "That wasn't funny," I told him. "How can that many people share one book?" He just chuckled and walked away.

Ten minutes later, he came back, his book open to where I had signed. "Can you please add Behi *joon*?" he asked.

During its first year in Iran, *Atre Sombol, Atre Koj* won the Readers' Choice Award from a magazine for twentysome-things called *Chel Cherogh,* meaning "chandelier." The name refers to the magazine's goal, which is to bring light where it is needed.

I was invited to the awards ceremony in Tehran but could not attend. Instead, I recorded my acceptance speech over the phone. More than two thousand people attended the cere-mony honoring twelve artists. My acceptance speech was played over a loudspeaker. Mohammad, without whose skills my stories would not exist in Iran, accepted the award on my behalf.

The magazine also requested a picture of me wearing a *hijab,* or headscarf. I tucked my hair under a periwinkle pash-mina, put on more makeup than I usually wear, in order to compensate for the lack of hair, and stood in front of the Christmas tree while my eleven-year-old took a few pictures. Thanks to the magic of digital cameras and e-mail, the photo reached Iran a few minutes later.

I asked the editor why he thought my book had become so popular with the young people in Iran. He said, "Your stories are funny, but the way you write about nationalities—you don't make one bad and one good. We don't hate Ameri-cans," he said. He told me that he wanted Americans to know this.

"I'll tell them that," I said.

Mommy, There's a Monkey on the Balcony

When I was six years old my father was transferred to Tehran for one year. I had known only one home in Abadan my entire life, and moving out of it was the saddest day of my six-year-old existence.

It wasn't the house itself that I loved so much; it was the garden. For as long as I could remember, I started each day in the garden, and each day, without exception, something had changed from the day before. No one had ever told me about gnomes or garden fairies, but they didn't have to. I witnessed firsthand the magic that happened every night as I slept; tomatoes ripened overnight, flowers opened upon mutual consensus, and swarms of insects appeared from where, I never knew. But that's not all. There was mystery where I could not see. Radishes grew big and red underground, and carrots lengthened over many nights. To see any of these changes required time and silence, two things I had in abundance. From my daily lengthy visits to the garden, I learned that the little things in life, those things we are most apt not to see, hold the most joy. I also knew, with utmost certainty, that there was something bigger than me in the world, and I knew it was something wonderful, much better than a gnome, elf, or garden fairy.

In Tehran, we moved into an apartment, which I hated instantly. There were more cars on our busy street than I could count. In Abadan, whenever I saw a car on our street, I knew whose it was. Tehran was full of strangers who were always in a hurry. The buildings were lit up all the time. The noise never stopped. The city was missing an Off button.

Despite round-the-clock activity in the streets, life in Tehran was very boring. I could no longer wander by myself for hours, lost in my thoughts. My entire roaming ground consisted of a tiny apartment with its tiny balcony. It's no wonder I hate zoos.

I was bored to tears every day, and whenever I complained my mother suggested I help her in the kitchen. This meant sitting in front of a large tray full of lentils, garbanzo beans, or mung beans and picking out the pebbles. I was very good at this, and my mother's praise made me enjoy the challenge of finding every single pebble, an activity that for my own children would be considered a punishment.

The excitement of cleaning legumes, however, was nothing compared to a surprise discovery I made one day, just like that of Christopher Columbus, albeit not as historically significant. I had finished cleaning the garbanzo beans when my mother suggested I pursue one of my favorite hobbies, dusting. I loved to dust. In Abadan, I used to follow our maid around. Tissue in hand, I would redust whatever she had already dusted. This I did for several reasons. I did not feel that our maid got all the nooks and crannies, nor did she always pick up objects to clean *under* them. I didn't feel she cared enough. She was a lackluster duster. I, on the other hand, viewed cleaning as a battle between good and evil. With every sweep of my tissue, I was annihilating the enemy. Although Abadan was famous for its abundant oil reserves, what it had more than anything was dust, making cleaning a truly satisfying experience. I'm also guessing I probably had some sort of mild disorder, that judging by the state of my house now, I've overcome, unfortunately.

I started cleaning in our apartment and, as always, picked up the phone to wipe the receiver. Suddenly, I heard voices. Even though nobody was using the phone, there were voices without owners having a conversation. Frozen with fear, I just stood there, not knowing what to do. Suddenly, as if the mysterious voices could now see me, one of them said, "Please put down the phone!"

I immediately slammed the phone. Convinced I had just experienced ghosts, I ran to my mother to try to describe to her what had just happened.

"*Maman!* There are people on the phone, *be khoda,* I swear to God!"

Without looking up from what she was doing, my mother said, "We have a shared phone line."

I had never heard of such a thing. Like everything else in Tehran, it made no sense to me.

My mother calmly explained that all three floors of our apartment building shared the same phone line. In Tehran, private lines took years to install and required paying bribes to everyone involved. Since we would be in Tehran for only one year, my mother explained that it wasn't worth trying to obtain our own line.

Perhaps in restrained cultures where people talk less, maybe Norway, shared phone lines might work. In Tehran, however, whenever my mother wanted to use the phone, somebody was already on it, having the most important conversation of his life. This was apparent because no matter how many times my mother picked up the receiver, which in most places means "I need to use the phone," nothing happened. It was understood that unless it was an emergency, the person wanting to make a phone call would never actually say anything, that the clicking of the receiver was enough to relay the message "your jaw muscles need to rest."

Then there was the issue of the phone ringing for somebody else. If we picked up the phone, and it wasn't for us, we had to tell the caller to please call back. Answering machines did not exist, so if the desired person was not home, this meant the phone just rang and rang and rang. This usually led to my dad yelling at the phone, "They're not home!"

But the peaceful scenario didn't end there. Sometimes after we had inadvertently picked up the phone and then hung up so the intended party could pick up, the phone would ring again and again and again. Eventually, we picked it up again, knowing it wasn't for us, but it was either that or hurling the phone off the balcony. The annoying caller would then plead with us to knock on the neighbor's door. "I don't know why she's not answering!" the caller would say in a worried voice. We then, being simple Abadanis perhaps, went up or down the stairs and knocked on the intended's door. Usually they weren't home, which is generally why people don't answer their phones. The one time they were home, we discovered that the "emergency" the caller had in mind consisted of a discussion about a hair appointment. From then on, if we were asked to serve as phone messengers, we either stomped on the floor or hit the ceiling with a broomstick.

I really missed my garden.

One day, bored as usual, I decided to see if anyone was on the phone. I knew this was probably not a good thing to do, but when has that stopped anyone? I gently picked up the receiver and, sure enough, a conversation. Just as I was figuring out what the conversation was about, one of the women said, "*Bebakhsheed,* excuse me, the phone is in use."

Having discovered that the voices belonged to mere mortals and not ghosts, I was no longer afraid. I kept listening. "Put down the phone please!" the voice said. I wanted to listen. After a minute or so, the women hung up the phone. There was a knock on our door.

My mother opened the door. It was our upstairs neighbor. "*Bebakhsheed,* excuse me, but I was just on the phone and someone was listening from your apartment." My mother was shocked. "I was nowhere near the phone. I was in the kitchen!" she exclaimed. "Maybe it was your daughter," the neighbor suggested, craning her neck to see as much of our apartment as she could. "She's only six," my mother said, obviously insulted by this intrusive woman. "You don't think she could have been listening?" the neighbor persisted, surveying the Persian rug in our entryway. My mo momentarily speechless. "Of course not! She is a girl and a very good student. She has been doi work in her room." This was true. I *had* be work, until I had decided to listen to the pl

Sherlock Holmes would have quit, but not this rubber-necked woman. "I hope it doesn't happen again. We never had this problem before you moved in."

My mother was on the verge of tears. She shut the door and went to call my father, but the phone was in use. When my father came home that night, my mother told him that she had forgotten how mean big-city people were. My father wanted to confront this outrageous neighbor, but my mother talked him out of it.

Forget the garden. I had found a much better hobby.

From then on, every free moment I had, I listened. The neighbors complained a few more times, but they eventually gave up. Every once in a while, though, as I listened to a conversation, one of the speakers would say, "There is something I will have to tell you later, in person, since there is *obviously* somebody listening to this conversation, somebody who should have the decency to hang up and not listen to what is not her business." I never took it personally. I had no TV, games, after-school activities, or playmates. It was either the phone or playing with matches. Luckily for the other tenants, I was afraid of fire.

Listening to people's candid conversations cut to their core. I found out the upstairs neighbor had something bad to say about everyone. Mrs. Bahmani's rice was always sticky, and Mrs. Tabrizi's *khoresht-e bademjun* was too salty. Elaheh *joon*'s seamstress did a sloppy job on her clothes, and Mani-jeh and Khosrow were having marital problems. The neighbor knew this because Manijeh had told her, but she wasn't sup-
~ed to tell anyone so please don't tell anyone, the neighbor
~alf the time, I could barely control myself from com-
~Stop going to Mrs. Bahmani's house if you hate her
~" I had fantasies of running into Manijeh and

telling her never again to tell a secret to my upstairs neighbor. Of course I would also tell Manijeh to try to make things work with Khosrow since, from what I'd heard, he was the best man she could ever hope for, with that complexion of hers and everything.

Our upstairs neighbor used the phone more than the rest of us combined. She had no life.

Our downstairs neighbor's conversations were nowhere as interesting, especially when the husband talked. He was all business. "What time will you be there? I'll be there at six. If I'm late, it's because of traffic. Traffic can be bad then." He was the only tenant who never complained about my listening. His conversations were so dull that he was probably grateful that someone out there was bored enough to listen to him.

When my father came home in the evening, I could no longer listen. My mother never noticed my listening since she was always in the kitchen, but my father would have noticed. Since they periodically had to defend me from neighbors' accusations, it was vital that they not see me for who I really was.

Every evening after dinner, my parents and I sat on the balcony while my brother Farshid did his homework in his room. Farshid attended a prestigious school that assigned so much homework that I never saw him anymore. My eldest brother, Farid, had not come with us to Tehran. He had gone to the United States to live with my uncle Mohammad Ali and his American wife, Linda.

The balcony was tiny, but after dinner every night my parents and I squeezed in for our daily dose of excitement. We lived across the street from the police department, and every evening was a reality show. This being Iran and not Norway, the people who came to the police department were expressive and loud. People fought and swore and insulted one another's mothers. Really angry people used their hands so much that spoken language seemed like an unnecessary accessory. When the traffic wasn't too loud, we could hear the conversations, since most of the action took place in front of the police station. Sometimes we took the sides of the people, such as the members of a wedding party who were arrested for excessive honking. Seeing a bride and groom all dressed up and swearing was way more exciting than anything I remembered from Abadan. I couldn't understand why they had been arrested, since all wedding parties honk, but my father explained that they were probably rich, and the officer just wanted a bribe. My mother said that maybe one of the officers was in love with the bride and he was trying to keep the wedding from happening. My father said that was the least likely scenario since, judging from the way that woman swore, her father must be rich to be able to get rid of her. I didn't have an explanation but I knew that if the upstairs neighbor were watching, I would hear *her* theory the next day, along with a description of the wedding dress and why it was not flattering.

One Friday morning, the only day of the week that Iranians do not work or attend school, I went into our kitchen and there, staring at me from the balcony, was a monkey. I recognized the monkey right away. He belonged to a local organ grinder who walked up and down our neighborhood collecting change while this poor monkey was forced to wear an unflattering jacket-and-fez ensemble made of crushed red velvet. The monkey didn't dance or perform in any way. He was merely dressed like Liberace and kept on a leash. I hated the organ grinder but absolutely loved the monkey. That's because I had a soft spot for monkeys.

My favorite toy ever was a stuffed monkey that had been given to me when I was born. If as a child someone had asked me whom I loved more, my brothers or my monkey, I would have found an excuse not to answer that question. I spent every day with my stuffed monkey, Maymoon, talking to it and telling it every thought that ever entered my head. I had agonized over its name because I could never decide if it was a she or a he. I finally decided to avoid that question by naming it Maymoon, which simply means "monkey" in Persian.

I still have Maymoon. She no longer has any fur, and all her limbs and one ear have fallen off at least once and been reattached. She's not pretty anymore, and I'm not sure she ever was. Her looks can best be summarized by my husband's remark when we first moved in together: "Put it somewhere where I don't have to look at it."

When the real monkey showed up on our balcony, it was by far the most exciting day of my life. I knew for certain that the monkey had chosen me because he knew that I loved him and his entire species. I envisioned Maymoon and the real monkey and myself living happily ever after together. As I went to open the door to the balcony, my father yelled, "*Nakon!* Don't do that!"

"But I want to hold him!" I told my father.

The monkey, meanwhile, was standing erect and pounding on our glass balcony door, shrieking.

"He's a wild, diseased monkey!" my father yelled at me.

My parents firmly believed that every animal equaled an affliction and danger. Dogs carried rabies, flies meant sleeping sickness, horses kicked you in the head, and cats scratched out eyes. And now, apparently, this monkey was also diseased, although my father did not elaborate.

I started to cry. My greatest wish, which I had not even thought of wishing, had come true and my own father, previously my favorite grown-up, was keeping me from fulfilling it. I wanted the monkey, and the monkey wanted me. I could see it in his face, although the shrieking part was not the stuff of fantasies.

In the meantime, my mother, who had come in the kitchen, kept telling my father to "do something." This really angered me since I could usually talk my father into doing anything I wanted, but once my mom came into the picture, all bets were off. I knew she would never allow me to keep the monkey in our apartment. That's just the kind of person she was.

I begged my father, "Please, please let me keep him!"

"Do something, Kazem!" my mother pleaded.

My father said, "Firoozeh, go look out the front window."

"No," I cried. "I just want to hug the monkey."

My father grabbed my hand and dragged me to their room. "Look," he said, pointing to the street below. A large crowd had formed in the street. In the middle stood the organ grinder, his hands in the air, crying and pleading to both his monkey and God. "The monkey does not belong to us," my father said. "We must try to help him leave our balcony. Plus, he's diseased."

Once I saw the sad organ grinder in the street, I knew that the monkey and I were doomed. "Let me just go look at him," I begged my father.

I went back to the kitchen where the little simian was still knocking on our balcony door. I fetched Maymoon and put it against the glass so they could see each other. The real monkey kept shrieking. Maymoon showed no reaction.

The monkey stayed on our balcony for three glorious hours. By the time his owner lured him down with food, our entire street was blocked due to the hundreds of people who had gathered to watch the scene, which, even by Tehran standards, was quite unusual.

From then on, whenever I saw the organ grinder, who now had the monkey on a much thicker rope, I felt like crying. The monkey and I had come *this* close to happily ever after. I wondered if the monkey remembered me. He never acknowledged me in an overt way, but I imagined that was probably because he was envious of Maymoon, who continues to grow old with me.

My Achilles' Meal

Every generation has its own style. One generation wears pants that are long and flared, the next prefers them pencil thin and to the ankle. One year, they're carefully hemmed, the next year, they're fringed.

Mourning, like pants, is also subject to styles. Of course, I am not referring to the actual act of dying since only God, and not the Gap, has a say in that. What changes from one generation to the next is how we react to death and how we explain it to our children.

When I was six years old, my maternal grandmother died. We didn't know she was sick. My mother found out through a dream. She dreamed that her father was very upset about something. This prompted my mother to call my grandfather, who reluctantly admitted that, indeed, my grandmother was in the hospital due to complications from diabetes. My mother and I flew to Tehran from Abadan. Two days later, my grandmother died.

As was the custom at the time, no one told me about her death. I knew that something was wrong, since kids pick up on anything parents try to hide, but I didn't know what death was, and nobody volunteered any information.

It was decided that the day of the funeral I would go to the house of my cousin Mahmood's new wife, Farah. Farah was a graduate student in chemistry who had met my cousin in college. They had been married for a few months. I had met her briefly at the wedding before I'd fallen asleep. I had, however, heard much about her, since every new addition to the family equaled hours and hours of tea-fueled gossip, speculation, and in-depth analysis, followed by more tea. Grown-ups always assumed that I, sitting by myself in a roomful of adults, was not listening, and even if I were, I would certainly not remember anything. Grown-ups are often wrong.

Farah was considered a great match for Mahmood. She was smart, well-traveled, and cultivated. Our families could not have been more different. Farah's family lived in a sprawling house in the Mahmoudieh section of northern Tehran. Their house was filled with books and artwork purchased during their travels abroad. It was, using the most complimentary contemporary word in Persian (though it's actually French), *chic*.

In addition, her house was surrounded by a large garden filled with cherry, peach, walnut, and (my all-time favorite fruit) mulberry trees. Their garden, like other private gardens in Tehran, was surrounded by a high wall, thus giving the whole place a magical quality for those of us lucky enough to be on the inside.

The day of the funeral, Farah picked me up early. I was

told that I would be spending the entire day with Mahmood's wife. This I found extremely strange since I had never spent the day with anybody but my parents. My apprehensions soon melted when Farah mentioned that we would first go toy shopping. I liked her immediately.

She took me to a department store in Tehran called Ferdowsi. My only experience shopping in stores was Alfi's in Abadan, and Ferdowsi was *much* bigger. We went to the toy section, which held more toys than I ever thought existed. Farah said, "I have finals tomorrow, so I need you to entertain yourself. Pick any toy you like."

I froze. There were too many choices. It was like the first time in the cereal aisle in an American supermarket. Farah quickly realized I needed help. She immediately picked a pink stroller with a ruffled top. Then she said, "Let's find a doll to put in it."

Once again, I was speechless. My father never, under any circumstance, bought me more than one toy per shopping trip. I assumed there was a law that set shopping limits. Little did I know that this rule existed only in my father's frugal kingdom.

Purchases in hand, we got into Farah's car. We drove through the busy streets, surrounded by more cars than I had ever seen, all honking at once to avoid one another or perhaps honking because the driver next to them was honking. Amid the cacophony, I was thinking about my new purchases and how I would have to point out to my parents that I had not *asked* for two toys. This was key.

Whenever I visited my grandfather, *baba bozorgh,* my mother always told me that if he ever asked me if I wanted any toys, I was to say, "No, thank you." I found this to be a stupid rule. Here was a grown-up *willing* to buy me a toy, and I was to say no. So I did what any self-respecting, greedy kid would do. Whenever my grandfather asked me if I wanted any toys, I always said, "No, thank you," just as I was supposed to. But then, later in the conversation, I would say, "*Baba bozorgh,* I really like those life-size inflatable elves, but I don't want one." This way, when my mother picked me up, along with my new life-size inflatable elf, I could honestly tell her that I had not asked for it. In fact, I had told *baba bozorgh* I didn't want it.

When we arrived at Farah's, a very friendly woman wearing a chador greeted us. The woman made a very strong first impression on me. She was tiny and ancient, far older than anyone I knew. But, more impressively, she was missing most of her teeth. I had seen babies with no teeth, but never a grown-up. When she kissed me, it tickled my cheek.

And this is how I was introduced to Khaleh Tavoos, or Aunt Peacock. She was not really Farah's aunt. Tavoos's mother had been Farah's grandmother's maid, and Tavoos had lived with Farah's family her entire life. She was a beloved member of their household.

Farah later told me that Tavoos claimed that the secret to her longevity was eating sugar. Several times a day, she poured some sugar in the palm of her hand and ate it straight. Farah's parents had purchased an expensive set of custom dentures for her, which she refused to wear, claiming she didn't need teeth to eat sugar, and sugar's all she needed. She lived to be ninety-two.

That day, Tavoos took me by her shriveled little hand and told me that she was so happy that I would be spending the day with her. She asked me if I wanted anything to eat.

No matter what time of the day you go into the home of an Iranian, you will be offered food. It can be one hour after you have consumed a wildebeest, but the host will still ask you. You can be bloated, lying on the floor, clutching your extended gut, top button of your pants burst open, but the host will still offer you food or drink "for your particular condition." We are people who need to feed people.

"No, thank you," I said. Then Tavoos said, "Would you like *seeb zamini sorkh kardeh*?" my all-time-favorite food, which my mother never made for me: French fries. Even though I wasn't hungry, French fries do not require hunger, only taste buds. "Yes, please," I said.

This made Tavoos genuinely happy. She disappeared into the kitchen while I went into an adjoining room to play with my new toys. But for the first time in my life I was not all that interested in my new toys. Being in this gigantic house with a toothless woman who wanted to make me French fries was more exciting than anything, even the revolutionary concept of two new toys on the same day.

Soon I heard sizzling noises as a heavenly smell wafted through the house. The stronger the smell, the more insignificant the stroller and doll became. By the time Tavoos walked in with a plate stacked high with French fries, I was ready to abandon my toys by the side of a road.

Tavoos placed the plate in front of me, then proceeded to sprinkle salt on the mountain of potatoes. The salt clung to the steamy stack. I could barely contain myself, but the potatoes were too hot. This was like child torture.

(I confess. I did manipulate my grandfather into buying me the life-size inflatable elf.)

The potatoes were still hot. Tavoos picked up one of the pieces of fried perfection and started blowing on it. Then she handed it to me. At my house, when someone cooled down a food, they ate it themselves. I had stumbled upon a full-service paradise.

I started to eat the French fries, which were not too greasy, perfectly crisp, and just salty enough. I must have been eating them with zeal, because as Tavoos sat staring at me with her toothless smile, she said, "Firoozeh *joon,* you must *really* like French fries." I wasn't sure why she was stating the obvious, so I nodded and kept eating.

I ate them all. Tavoos smiled even more broadly and asked me if I wanted more.

I had entered an alternate universe. Never had anyone offered to make French fries just for me, and now this woman was asking me the inconceivable.

"Yes, please," I said, hoping the second batch wouldn't take as long.

Tavoos adjusted her chador and went into the kitchen. Soon the sizzling noises began again and smells filled the house. I glanced at the stroller and doll, which looked even less interesting than before. Compared with a plate of French fries, the only way the doll would have had a chance with me would have been if she had started talking, or making French fries.

After what seemed like an eternity, Tavoos walked in with a plate stacked high with freshly fried potatoes and sat across from me. She salted them, took a fry, and started blowing on it. This time, I knew it was for me. It's amazing how quickly one adjusts to fine service.

As I finished the second plate, Tavoos beamed and asked me if I wanted more. I didn't know the phrase *carpe diem* back then, but I lived by it. And to me, seizing the day meant eating more French fries.

Somehow, the smells weren't as enticing the third time. When Tavoos brought the plate of fries, I waited for them to cool and started eating considerably more slowly than the other two times. Tavoos continued to smile.

Halfway through the plate, I just couldn't finish the stack. "What's the matter?" Tavoos asked. "I feel sick," I told her. She led me to an empty bedroom where I lay down, moaning and groaning. "Maybe you ate too many French fries," she said.

"I don't think so," I replied.

I lay down for the rest of the afternoon. Tavoos repeatedly offered to make me various concoctions to make my stomach feel better.

"Tea with *nabat,* crystallized sugar?" she suggested.

"No, thank you," I replied.

"*Sharbat-e ablimu ba naana?* Fresh lime-aid with mint?"

"No, thank you."

"*Sharbat-e albalu?* Sour cherry syrup?"

"No, thank you."

"*Dugh?* Carbonated yogurt drink?"

"No, thank you."

"Seven-Up?"

"No, thank you."

Tavoos sat next to me telling me stories and stroking my hair. I couldn't listen to a word she was saying. My stomach felt as if I had swallowed the doll's stroller.

A few hours later, Farah returned home and was shocked to find me lying down. "*Chi shodeh?* What happened?" she asked.

"Firoozeh *joon* ate three plates of French fries," Tavoos said, making me sound like some kind of glutton.

"Why did you let her eat so much?" Farah asked, clearly

not grasping the gravitational pull of fried potatoes on this particular six-year-old.

"She wanted them," Tavoos replied, underestimating my total lack of common sense in selecting healthy portion sizes. It is the same glitch that compels otherwise sane Americans to proudly declare, "Supersize it."

Farah gathered up my new toys while Tavoos kissed me and told me how much she'd enjoyed spending the day with me. She hugged me tightly and told me repeatedly to make sure I visit her again, probably making a mental note to lock the pantry.

On the drive home, Farah apologized for not having had more time to play with me. She told me that her final exams tomorrow were very important, and maybe we could play together another time.

We arrived to a houseful of sad adults, all trying to conceal their sorrow from me. I showed everyone my stroller and doll, but left out the part about Khaleh Tavoos and the never-ending perfect French fries. It didn't seem right to share that with this crowd. They needed to be sad. I knew that much.

Maid in Iran:

A Story in Three Parts

PART I: ALI SITTING IN A TREE

During the years my family lived in Abadan, like most middle-class Iranian families, we had full-time help. In Iran, servants were usually villagers who spent a few years living and working with families in the cities. They sometimes returned to their villages with their savings and raised their children surrounded by their extended families. Other times, servants stayed for life and became a part of the family.

When my parents were married, the first two maids left after a few months, claiming the house was too boring. The real problem was that my parents were not very good with servants. My mother, having been brought up in a military home, had little experience with servants. During her childhood, the military supplied help for her house in the form of low-ranking personnel. But those servants knew what was expected of them; nobody needed to manage them.

Since my father was at work most of the day, my mother was left to the task of dealing with the help. Having married at age seventeen, she had little life experience. She relied mainly on the subtle hint approach. This entailed such methods as leaving a heap of dirty dishes in the kitchen and hoping really hard that the maid would wash them. This method did not work.

After the first two servants left, my parents hired a couple, Ali and Zahra, from the city of Arak in west central Iran. In the Persian culture, we often say that most things in life take three tries, and it was certainly true in this case. Zahra turned out to be a take-charge kind of person—reliable, competent, and smart. Her husband, Ali, was her counterpoint. Having married a strong and capable woman, he allowed himself the luxury of being neither. Ali's only apparent talent was climbing trees, a skill that he practiced regularly. Whenever we couldn't find him, which was often, we'd look up, and there he was, resting on a branch. It soon became evident to my parents that having Ali was the price they had to pay for having Zahra.

When my mother became pregnant with my brother Farshid, she relied on Zahra even more. My mother always said that it was a cruel twist of fate that Zahra had been born poor, since she was a true lady and deserved much more in life than being a maid. My parents regarded Zahra as family, always inviting her and, by extension, Ali to eat at the dining room table with us. Zahra always accepted. Ali always declined.

My parents lived a comfortable middle-class life but were never wealthy. The few valuables they once owned, namely silver from my mother's family, they sold during the early years of their marriage, when money was scarce. The one and only valuable object they possessed was my father's 1953 yearbook from Texas A&M. We treated this item like a biblical relic, showing it to guests while my father recounted, in excruciating detail, how he won a Fulbright scholarship even though he was poor, how well he had been treated in America, how he had met Albert Einstein, how many colors of Jell-O there were in the cafeteria, and how, in America, people put ice in tea. The latter always caused incredulous outbursts. "Ice in tea?! Not possible," our guests always said, shaking their heads in disbelief.

Even though everyone had heard my father's Fulbright story many, many times, no one ever tired of it. Each recounting was delivered with the same near-religious fervor. Had my father been a salesman making a pitch, he would have sold out of whatever he was selling. At certain parts in the tale, my father's eyes would well up with tears. This was the time my mother would offer another round of tea to the guests, who usually did not appreciate the interruption. They, too, were swept away by my father's story.

At the end of the tale, my father would then show everyone the yearbook, which served as proof that at least the major part of his story was true. Unfortunately, there were no pictures of ice tea in his yearbook.

One day, my father discovered that his yearbook was missing. He knew it could not have been stolen, since it held no value for others. He assumed it would show up somewhere. Catholics pray to St. Anthony for lost objects. We don't have the equivalent in Islam, so my father just waited.

A few months later, Ali and Zahra invited my parents to their room for tea and sweets to celebrate the Iranian New

Year. Ali and Zahra's room was separate from our house, in the back of the garden. My parents never went there.

Gifts in hand, my parents walked in, ready to deliver the compliments that are second nature to us Middle Easterners. But before any niceties could spill from their mouths, though, they were rendered speechless. Staring at them, from all the four walls of Ali and Zahra's room, were the women of Texas A&M. Individual head shots, club poses, photos of librarians—they were all there, each carefully cut out and taped to the wall. Granted, my father's yearbook was no *Playboy* magazine. These were pictures of studious, smart women, trailblazers paving the way for equality. But they were from *Amrika* and therefore exotic. Little did these students, teachers, and librarians from 1953 know that somewhere on the other side of the world, in a room in the back of a house in Abadan, they were now wallpaper.

My father knew there was not much to be done at this point. He couldn't fire Ali since Zahra was the first helpful servant we had ever had. He decided, instead, to find Ali a job elsewhere.

One of my father's former students was the manager of the local clubhouse. The entire Middle East operates on the premise of who you know, so my father decided to pay his former student a visit, drink some tea, and remind him how he would have flunked his course had it not been for my father's tutoring services. My father figured that the clubhouse, with its theater, pool, and restaurant, could certainly use a person with Ali's tree-climbing skills.

Once my father walked into his former student's office, he skipped the tea and simply said, "I have a useless servant. Certainly your clubhouse needs someone." Not long after, Ali was hired as a sort of Man Friday.

It just so happened that this clubhouse manager had a habit of going into his office during his lunch hour, closing the door, turning on his radio, putting his feet on his desk, and eating the Cadbury chocolates he hid in his top drawer.

Ali had been employed for one month when my father received an angry phone call from his friend. It turns out he had walked into his office to find Ali sitting in his chair, feet on the desk, listening to the radio, and eating Cadbury chocolates. Ali was fired.

There was nothing my parents could do. They were too fond of Zahra to get rid of them both. By then, Zahra had become a regular at our dinner table. She was family. My mother had even bought her a sewing machine.

One day, my brother Farid, who was a toddler, wandered into Ali and Zahra's room and waddled back to the house holding a letter. Most people would simply have returned the unread letter to its owner and explained the situation, but Kazem and Nazireh are not most people. They read the letter, which was from Ali and Zahra's relatives in Arak.

Dear Ali and Zahra,
You have so much money now. Come home and live the
good life! Make sure to take the sewing machine.

My parents were in a pickle.

The next day, my parents told Zahra, "The sewing machine is a gift to you. You can keep it forever." My parents were hoping that their oblique approach would lead to a conversation. It didn't.

Ali and Zahra continued receiving letters from their relatives. My parents were anxious to find out the contents of the letters. They encouraged Farid to wander in the yard, always pointing him toward Ali and Zahra's room. Unfortunately my brother's usefulness as a spy was a onetime affair.

Eventually, Ali and Zahra told my parents that they had decided to return to Arak. My parents pleaded with them to stay, but Ali was convinced that with their savings, they would buy a house and live comfortably for the rest of their lives. My father tried to explain to him that it would be much harder to find a well-paying job in Arak and that their savings would not buy them as much as they thought. But it was useless. Much to my parents' regret, Ali and Zahra left, taking with them the sewing machine and the Women of Texas A&M wallpaper.

PART II: REZA AND SAKINEH SITTING IN A TREE

Once again, my parents went in search of a servant. This time, they hired a young woman, Sakineh, who had been introduced to them through a friend in Tehran. Unbeknownst to my parents, Sakineh was pregnant.

Shortly after Sakineh moved in with us, my aunt Sedigeh needed to go to England for six months for medical treatment. She asked that we please employ her servant Reza during her absence, but told my parents repeatedly, however, "Don't ruin him. I've had him for only a few months."

My aunt Sedigeh, who herself is highly disciplined, was quite adept at teaching her workers actually to work. She viewed servants as blank slates with endless possibilities. She spent hours teaching them the proper ways of cleaning and taking care of the garden and fixing things around the house. For the ones who showed more talent, she found teachers to instruct them on how to fix plumbing and bicycles and radios and anything else that might need repairing. She even taught them manners, especially how to greet people and the proper way to answer the phone. She was Abadan's own Pygmalion.

As soon as my aunt Sedigeh left for England, my parents asked Reza to come to our house to help with our vegetable garden. Reza quickly summed up my parents and realized that he was no longer at Sedigeh Academy. He spent hours in the garden with no visible proof of accomplishing anything. Every hour, he came in the house for a cup of tea, and every afternoon, when everyone else napped, he somehow disappeared. My parents didn't like the fact that he wasn't doing much, but as poster children for meek people everywhere, they decided to let my aunt deal with it when she returned.

Between avoiding weeding the vegetable garden and neglecting to clean the chicken cages, Reza fell in love with Sakineh. My parents didn't figure this out themselves; the information came courtesy of a neighbor. Apparently every evening, Reza and Sakineh went to the nearby port town of Khoramshahr, rented a *balam,* or rowboat, and spent the evening doing what one does on a date in a rowboat. It became obvious that in lieu of weeding, Reza had been wooing.

By the time my parents found out about the Love Boat, Reza and Sakineh's love, like the weeds in our garden, was in full bloom. To complicate matters, my parents had also noticed that Sakineh was pregnant, and it was obvious by how far along she was that Reza was not the only man who had rowed her boat.

My aunt Sedigeh was scheduled to return from England shortly, and my parents were beside themselves. Aunt Sedigeh was my father's beloved older sister, who had raised him after the death of their mother. He never wanted to upset her. For my mother, Aunt Sedigeh was the closest thing she had to a mother-in-law. No need to say more.

In the weeks prior to my aunt's return, my parents argued incessantly. My father blamed my mother for not keeping a watchful eye on the servants, while my mother blamed my father for the same thing.

When my aunt returned, my parents went to her house to welcome her back home, and my aunt asked how Reza had been. In the Persian culture, questions are rarely answered directly, so my parents hemmed and hawed and drank some tea, and then my father explained that Reza had been fine. In fact, he had been so fine that Sakineh had noticed his fineness.

"You obviously didn't give him enough work," my aunt assessed.

"Maybe," my father continued, drinking more tea. "But now with the baby due any day, he will have much more work."

It's not clear where the conversation went after that. There are several versions.

The following week, my aunt, angry and practical at the same time, purchased a ring for Reza to give to Sakineh, and the two of them wed in my aunt's garden in a five-minute ceremony. Once they were married, Sakineh moved into my aunt's house and prepared to give birth.

Reza's family refused to come to the wedding once they found out that his fiancée was pregnant with another man's child. They were certain that the eligible Reza had been hoodwinked by the she-devil herself. Sakineh's family was not told about the wedding until afterward, since they would not have looked kindly upon their daughter's baklava in the oven.

My aunt kept telling us that she would have never believed

that in a mere six months we could have so thoroughly ruined her servant. "Maybe I should have been more specific: 'Make sure he does not fall in love with your already pregnant maid.' "

"Next time," my father promised, "this will not happen."

PART III: DING DING

My parents' search for servant number four brought us an entire family: Pooran, her husband Ahmad, their three daughters, Pooran, Pari, and Parvaneh, and their infant son, Parviz. Ahmad called himself Kal Ahmad, using the prefix earned by men after visiting Karbala, the holy city in Iraq where Imam Hussein was killed in the year 680. His wife, Pooran, was called Naneh Pooran; *naneh* is a term of endearment meaning nanny or housekeeper.

By the time our new servants joined us, my family had moved into a larger house, with a mini house in the back for household help. Since all our homes had been designed by the British for the British, many had servants' quarters, servants being one of the perks in colonialism.

With the arrival of Naneh Pooran and Kal Ahmad's family, my parents suddenly found themselves surrounded by children. My mother immediately went shopping. She bought dresses, shoes, and school bags. The joy of receiving new clothing is universal, and for all the years they lived with us, my mother shopped for Naneh Pooran and Kal Ahmad's children. By just looking at the kids in our house, no one could ever tell whose were the maid's and whose were the owners'. That is exactly what my parents wanted. My mother still says that had she known how much she would enjoy shopping for

Pooran, Pari, Parvaneh, and Parviz, she would have hired servants with children much sooner.

Our house was on an acre of land. This was not as luxurious as it sounds. Abadan, with its desert climate and ubiquitous oil refineries, is no Manhattan. We lived in a one-story house with three bedrooms, similar to what Americans call "ranch-style." Our front yard was filled with flowers, and the backyard had a vegetable garden and chicken coop. Kal Ahmad was in charge of everything outside the house, and Naneh Pooran took care of everything inside. They were both seasoned servants, and our house ran smoothly with their help.

A few months after Naneh Pooran and her family moved in with us, we received a letter from Ali and Zahra. They had returned to Arak, where various family members had swindled them of all their money and belongings, even Zahra's sewing machine. They begged my parents to take them back. My parents couldn't, but promised to help them find jobs. My father finally found a job for Ali as an elevator operator in a hospital in Tehran. It somehow seemed fitting that Ali, who spent his days going up and down trees, would now spend his days going up and down in an elevator.

One day my father came home to find Kal Ahmad with his face in his hands, sobbing. Turns out someone had stolen his bicycle, his sole mode of transportation. Seeing people cry happens to be my father's kryptonite. This weakness served me well as a child, leading to the acquisition of many toys.

My father told Kal Ahmad to get in the car, and the two of them drove to the bicycle shop, where my father proceeded to buy Ahmad the nicest top-of-the-line bike he could find. He even bought him a bell.

Kal Ahmad loved the bell. He rang it as he left the house.

He rang it as soon as he turned into our driveway. He rang it whenever he saw someone he knew. He rang it just for fun. Every time we'd hear the familiar ding, ding, ding, my dad would say, "I should not have bought that bell."

Every evening, Naneh Pooran and Kal Ahmad invited my four-year-old brother Farshid to join them for dinner, and Farshid happily accepted. Naneh Pooran and her family ate their dinner sitting on the floor, which Farshid found more enjoyable than sitting at our dining room table. And more important, they always offered him the *tadig* first. *Tadig* is the crispy fried rice at the bottom of the pan, the most coveted part of a Persian meal. No matter how big the pot, there is only a limited amount of *tadig*. This means that at any Persian meal, everyone grabs the *tadig* first. It's *Lord of the Flies*. For Naneh Pooran and her family to offer Farshid the *tadig* first every night was the height of generosity. Their son, Parviz, and Farshid were playmates, but when it came time to eat, Farshid *agha,* or Mr. Farshid, as they called him, was treated like the boss's son.

When Farshid was ready to start school, my parents faced a huge dilemma. In Iran, like in most countries in the world, if your daddy's a gardener, you'll be a gardener, too. If you're a complete idiot from a wealthy family, you will have access to all types of educational and job opportunities. My father always said that had Albert Einstein been born to a poor Iranian family, the world would have never benefited from his gifts because he would have been stuck plowing a field somewhere. My father also added that having met Albert Einstein, he felt personally strong about this issue. This casual name-dropping elicited awe every time, allowing my father to segue to his Fulbright Scholarship story, complete with "I did not think I was going to win" and "They put ice in tea, I swear."

When it was time for Farshid to attend school, my parents enrolled him in the school for employees of the National Iranian Oil Company. Parviz, on the other hand, had to attend the public school, where his sisters went. The problem was that the public school started at age six, while Farshid's school started at age five. My parents did not want Parviz to have to watch my brother leave for school while he sat at home. My father was not an influential enough man to persuade the public school to bend the rule, but he had friends who were. He made a few phone calls, and Parviz was allowed to start school the same year as my brother.

In the evenings, my father personally saw to it that Parviz did all his homework correctly. Whenever Parviz had a question, he came to my father, since his own father was illiterate.

Naneh Pooran and Kal Ahmad lived with us until my father received a two-year assignment to come to America. They were devastated. Nobody cried harder at the news than they did. Even though my parents found them another family in Abadan, Naneh Pooran and Kal Ahmad insisted that they would never find another employer who treated them like family.

My parents stayed in touch with Parviz. When he finished high school, my father enrolled him in a technical training program. When he graduated, my father arranged a job interview for him. He was hired as a technician at the National Iranian Oil Company, where he still works. He and his wife and kids live in a house in Abadan.

Parviz did not grow up to be a gardener.

And I grew up believing that one person can make a difference.

Eight Days a Week

When I met my first teacher in America, Mrs. Sandberg, I was so confused. She was so *nice*. Her classroom was unlike anything I had ever seen—colorful posters on the walls, children's artwork hanging from the ceiling; it was like a party. Mrs. Sandberg never yelled, assigned homework, or even lost her temper, but she knew how to control the classroom. If someone misbehaved, she would say, "Jaimie, I need to speak to you," in a stern but still-kind tone. Then she would speak to the student in question, in a logical way that assumed the existence of a higher self in even the worst of her students. If the student continued to misbehave, he would have to eat lunch in the classroom with Mrs. Sandberg instead of running around outside with his friends. The student in question would inevitably be sorry for whatever he had done. Mrs. Sandberg never hit anyone.

Every day after lunch, she read a book to us while we put our heads on our desks. I can still hear her soothing voice introducing me to Charlotte, Wilbur, and the Boxcar Children. When we finished our class assignments—which was the least we could do since we were, after all, students—she gave us stickers that read, "Nice Job!" or "You're a star!" Every so often, there was a party for someone's birthday or for some other reason, such as Arbor Day. These parties meant we received sweets and eraser heads. Not surprisingly, at the end of the year, I received an award for perfect attendance. I had not missed a single day of school, not because I was never sick but because I vehemently refused to stay home. Why would anyone miss a day of Mrs. Sandberg's class?

Mrs. Sandberg's scope did not stop in the classroom. Shortly after I started school, she called my father at home and told him that she had noticed that I loved books and that he needed to take me to the Whittier Public Library. As far as my father is concerned, the eleventh commandment is "Obey your children's teachers." He immediately told my brother Farshid to take me to the library. I grabbed my purse and off we went.

Even though my father's employer in Abadan, the National Iranian Oil Company, provided a well-stocked library, complete with a children's section, I had never been there because no one had ever taken me. My family was not much into reading for fun. They read what they had to in school, but beyond that, nada. In fact, I didn't know what a Library was until Mrs. Sandberg's fateful phone call.

As we walked to the Whittier Public Library, Farshid explained to me that a library is a place that lends books to people. I didn't argue because I was seven and he was fourteen, but I thought he was full of hooey. I knew enough to know that there was no place that lent things to people. That's why I had brought my purse.

In Iran, I owned three books: *Aesop's Fables, The Little Prince,* and the witty *Tales of Mullah Nasrudin,* all of which had been given to me by my uncle's wife, Soraya, who lived in Tehran and wore sophisticated clothes, ate fancy foods such as artichokes, and loved books. Those same three books are still among my top twenty favorites, although the original copies were lost a long time ago, somewhere between our first and twelfth move.

Perhaps it's not entirely fair to say that my parents were not into reading for fun. They did buy one book in America during the two years our family lived here, the 1972 edition of the *Guinness Book of World Records.* That book I still have, thanks to my mother, who recently gave it to me, with the explanation "We don't have room for this."

When Farshid and I arrived at the library, we went into a huge room filled with children's books. I had never seen so many books just for children in one place. I picked the smallest book, assuming it would be the cheapest. When I went to pay for it, coin purse in hand, the librarian made my brother fill out a sheet of paper; then she handed me a card with my name, Firoozeh Jazayeri, correctly spelled but barely fitting on the line provided. She then handed me the book I had chosen—for free. I was stunned. She was *lending* it to me. I thought then and there that libraries were the most brilliant idea ever and wondered who had thought of them. From then on, I went to the library every chance I had and checked out the maximum number of books allowed, eight. No matter how many books I read, there were always more, which both exhilarated and frustrated me.

Ever since we had arrived in the United States, my classmates kept asking me about magic carpets. "They don't exist," I always said. I was wrong. Magic carpets do exist, but they are called library cards.

School in Iran had been a whole other experience. We attended school six days a week; Fridays were our only day off, but we received enough homework to keep us busy eight days a week.

Starting from the first day of first grade, we had homework—hours of it. Our grading system was based on twenty points. Nineteens and twenties were very, very rare. Teachers were stern, feared, and respected. They very rarely complimented students; and when they did, you remembered it, and so did your parents and the other students.

When teachers entered a room, all the students stood up, in silence, and we didn't sit down again until the teacher said we could. Talking back was unheard of. Putting your feet up on the chair? Are you kidding? Chewing gum, eating, or chitchatting with a classmate? Never. We sat in rows in unadorned rooms, off unadorned hallways. And if I could send my children back in time to school in prerevolutionary Iran, I would.

Our teachers did not try to be our friends or to be liked. They were there to teach us. There were no birthday celebrations. Why should there be? I will never understand why most schools in America celebrate Halloween, effectively losing an entire day of education to prepare kids for collecting candy.

In Iran, we were graded on penmanship and neatness. Our pencils always had to be sharp. I still have a bump on my finger from doing endless writing exercises. We had math and science every day, hours in the classroom and more at home. When we studied plants, we had to draw various species, labeling each part. Our drawings had to be perfectly neat. We learned the difference between deciduous and evergreen, and what happens to plants during each season. We knew citrus fruit had eight sections. We knew the various kinds of seeds and pits. We knew the major cities in Iran, the capitals of other countries, the names of mountains and where to find them. If we didn't do well and pass these subjects, we flunked and had to repeat the year. Nobody wanted that.

And of course, we studied our heroes.

If you ask someone in Iran to name three famous countrymen, you'll probably hear Ferdowsi, Hafez, and Saadi. They were not military men, inventors, athletes, or rock stars, but poets.

Ferdowsi was a tenth-century poet, best known for *Shahnameh, The Epic of Kings,* which tells the story of old Persia before the Arab conquest. The poem is written entirely in Persian. Ferdowsi is credited with not only creating a masterpiece but helping preserve the Persian language by not using any words with Arabic roots. Some pages from an exquisite sixteenth-century *Shah-nameh* are on display at the Metropolitan Museum in New York. I visit those pages every time I am in New York and marvel at how one man could have written something that is as popular today as it was a thousand years ago. His awe-inspiring poems are reason enough for everyone to learn Persian.

In prerevolutionary Iran, every student had to memorize at least one of the poems of the beloved Saadi, a poet from the thirteenth century. One of Saadi's most famous poems, about shared humanity, is carved in the entrance of the Hall of Nations in the United Nations building in New York. When a poem from the strife-filled thirteenth century is equally relevant in the strife-filled twenty-first century, one wonders if we really are as gifted a species as we think we are. Sure, we've invented huge metal objects that can fly, or sit on runways for hours, and, yes, doctors can give one person's still-beating heart to another, and we have endless products to make straight hair curly and curly hair straight, but we still don't know how to get along. Perhaps Starbucks should start printing Saadi's poem on its cups, thus spreading the concept, with every shot of espresso sold around the world, that our commonalities far outweigh our differences.

Hafez, another prominent Iranian, was a fourteenth-century poet whose mystical poems are full of metaphors, lending themselves to all sorts of interpretations. Hafez's simple yet inimitable writing style has enchanted Iranians for centuries. No one has ever been able to write like him, despite many attempts. In our house, whenever a decision was to be made, my father would grab the book of poems by Hafez, close his eyes, ask a question, open a page at random, read the poem on that page, and interpret it with much wonder and awe. He does the same thing with fortune cookies in Chinese restaurants. I am continually amazed at how much he can read into "He who travels sees much" and "Your lucky numbers are 23 14 9 32 1."

Using Hafez's poems as some sort of divine guidance is common practice in many Iranian households, especially around potential suitors. Hafez has single-handedly encouraged many unions and prevented others. He is also often used as an excuse to reject a suitor, as opposed to "we're holding out for a doctor." I assume there are many Iranian men out there with grudges against Hafez.

In a strange intersection between modernity and tradition, there is even a Hafez website, in Persian, which allows the user to select a poem by clicking on one of the question marks covering the screen, then reading and interpreting the corresponding poem. I don't know how Hafez would have felt about the website, but its existence does prove that human beings are always looking for someone to provide answers to life's endless questions. We have Hafez; you have Dr. Phil. It is to be noted, however, that Hafez has been popular for seven centuries and gained prominence without the help of Oprah Winfrey.

In addition to Persian poets, the reading curriculum in pre-revolutionary Iran covered a wide range of foreign authors and philosophers. Depending on the school, students read the works of Dickens, Twain, Dostoyevsky, Gogol, Chekhov, Gorky, Nietzsche, Borges, Arthur Koestler, Stefan Zweig, Sartre, de Beauvoir, and Camus, to name a few. Hemingway was added in later years. We also had weekly magazine supplements that serialized Alexandre Dumas's novels *Joseph Balsamo* and *The Count of Monte Cristo*. These were very popular, proving that cliff-hangers succeed in every language.

In Abadan, the children of almost all employees of the National Iranian Oil Company attended the same schools. Parvaneh for kindergarten, Roya coed grammar school for grades one through three, then Babak for boys from grades four through six. Girls continued at Roya through high school; boys attended 25 Shahrivar.

In 1971, when we transferred to Tehran for one year, the culture shock of moving from Abadan was every bit as jarring as moving to America would later be. In addition to getting used to Tehran traffic, which meant brushing up on both prayers and swear words, my father had to decide where to send us to school.

In Tehran, the most prestigious school for boys was Alborz. Alborz was Iran's Eton, famous for having top teachers, hardworking students destined for success, and science labs that rivaled those of major universities. The principal was a man named Dr. Mojtahedi.

In 1968, as part of his job, Dr. Mojtahedi embarked on a tour of universities and refineries in Iran. At the time, my father worked for the National Iranian Oil Company and was assigned to host Dr. Mojtahedi during his visit. The two of them spent a couple of days together and got along splendidly. When it was time for him to return to Tehran, Dr. Mojtahedi told my father that if he ever came to Tehran, he should be sure to look him up. My father, displaying his usual social skills, said yes, and then proceeded to forget about Dr. Mojtahedi.

Three years later, when we moved to Tehran, my father decided that the only logical school choice for Farshid was Alborz. When he called the school to enroll him, he was told that my brother would have to take an entrance exam. My father suddenly remembered Dr. Mojtahedi. "Don't worry," he told my brother. "I'll take care of this."

The next day, my parents, Farshid, and I put on our finest clothes and went to Alborz. The school was empty and eerily quiet. My father asked the janitor where he could find Dr. Mojtahedi. The janitor pointed to a set of doors. The four of us, led by my intrepid father, opened the doors and walked into a huge room where hundreds of students sat hunched over desks, working feverishly, rapidly pushing pencils across stacks of paper. The silence was broken by the screams of a gray-haired man standing in the front of the room: "*Who* are you and *why* are you here?"

This was not the welcome my father had expected from Dr. Mojtahedi. After all, the principal had told my father to look him up next time he was in Tehran. He should have been more specific: "But don't barge in on our entrance exams."

We left immediately. My father, pretending not to be red-faced and covered with sweat, assured my brother that he would take care of it the next day. Farshid told my father that he had helped enough and to please never help him again.

Two weeks later, Farshid, along with another group of prospective students, took the school's entrance exam, in that same room, and was accepted.

There are currently literally tens of thousands of Alborz graduates in successful positions around the world. The school's principal, Dr. Mohammad Ali Mojtahedi, the gray-haired man who rightfully screamed at us, was a living legend. From a poor background, due to the lack of educational opportunities he did not finish high school until age twenty-two. As principal of Alborz, he was famous for being dedicated, protective, and incorruptible. He admitted students based on ability. Poor students with no connections or wealth studied alongside the sons of the rich and powerful, all of whom had been admitted for their academic abilities.

My brother was so fond of the rigorous culture at Alborz that, the following year, he wanted to stay in Tehran with relatives instead of coming with us to America. My parents, however, decided that he had to come along.

Like Farshid, I, too, experienced a private school in Tehran, albeit one of a different flavor. When we arrived in Tehran, I took an entrance exam for a coed school known for high academic standards. A few days later, my father received a phone call from the head of the school. "I'm sorry, Mr. Jaza-yeri," he said. "The test results are in, and your daughter is not gifted." After he hung up, my father called someone who knew someone who knew someone. The next day, he received another phone call from the head of the school. "Congratulations, Mr. Jazayeri," he said, "your daughter *is* gifted."

Despite the sometimes less-than-admirable admissions policy, I give credit to my Iranian schools for teaching me discipline. I learned that school meant work, not play. I never expected my teachers to make subjects fun. Fun was what I had with my friends, outside the classroom. Of course, the system was far from perfect. With absolute power, some teachers went too far. For example, corporal punishment was allowed. When my father's assignment in America ended in 1974, we moved to Ahwaz for six months. My teacher there took full advantage of the right to hit us. I thought then, and still think, that she was mentally unwell. The students she targeted were ones who did not do their work; perhaps they had learning disabilities or just needed more help. With the bar set high, it was easy to feel stupid and give up. Those kids would probably have blossomed in Mrs. Sandberg's classroom.

Judging from the number of successful Iranian immigrants scattered around the world after the revolution, it's easy to see that Iranian schools used to be quite good. I wish I could incorporate some of their high standards into my children's schools in America. But they would never work here. Kids would complain that lots of math drills are not fun, which is true. Parents would complain about the amount of homework. Having lots of homework is indeed inconvenient and requires organization and time-management skills, which kids do not have. This means that they must learn those skills, which is also not fun. And maybe that's the problem. Delayed gratification has fallen out of fashion. Good old Iranian or American qualities such as aiming high and striving despite difficulties have been replaced with everyone receiving a trophy for participating.

But that's not the only obstacle. In Iran, we celebrated the math geniuses, the ones with neat handwriting, the ones who tried to excel in school, the ones who spent a lot of time on their homework. They received prizes. Their names were in the newspaper. We applauded them and wished our children could be like them.

Here, those kids are called nerds and geeks and dorks. This may be the only country where people make fun of the smart kids. Now *that's* stupid. I only hope that the engineer who built the bridge I drive across or the nurse who administers our vaccines or the teacher who teaches my kids was a total nerd.

Thirty-five years after finishing second grade, I still keep in touch with Mrs. Sandberg. That alone qualifies me as a poster child for geeks, dorks, and nerds everywhere. Whenever we talk on the phone, Mrs. Sandberg insists that I call her by her first name, Bonnie. I can't do that.

What I can do is tell her that I appreciated what she taught me, which was very different from what I learned in my schools in Iran. She showed me that one sensitive educator could make a pivotal difference in a person's life. She also taught me how to make a planetarium out of a shoebox and track the stars.

May every student have a Dr. Mojtahedi or a Mrs. Sandberg.

June Joon

In 1974, during what must have been an uneventful period in American history, my family and I were featured in the local Whittier newspaper under the caption "Ambassadors Sans Portfolio." The article was accompanied by a large photo of my parents, my brother Farshid, and me, sitting on our sofa looking at each other in a smiley way that, prior to the presence of the photographer in our living room, had never, ever occurred before. For this special occasion, I had donned my polyester pants and sweater combo from Sears. The outfit was a size fourteen Pretty Plus. There's nothing green about Greenland and there was nothing pretty about Pretty Plus. I assumed that fourteen Ate-Too-Much-Kentucky-Fried-Chicken would not fit on the tag.

Right next to our photo was a column by a Ms. Shirley Ruth, who doled out decorating advice. On that particular day in history, a Mrs. K. Potter had written her a long, detailed letter pleading for help: "Can you help us decorate our rather large living room? The carpet is a cut pile in a light cream color . . . my biggest problem is the layout of the room and placement of colors." Mrs. Potter's cry for help was answered with an even longer and more detailed letter involving "U-shaped sectionals," "cream-colored rayon satin tassels," and "celery green striped fabric with rows of miniature yellow-and-melon-colored flowers with tiny celery green leaves."

The journalist assigned to interview us was a woman by the name of June, which means "dear" in Persian. Dear June started with the usual questions about how long we had been there and what we thought of America. My father, droning in the monotone that he always saved for Americans, told her about his Fulbright Scholarship, his grant from the Ford Foundation, and the oil industry. He then delivered his "Iran is not an Arab country" speech, followed by his "Shah's plans to industrialize Iran" speech, and topped it with his soliloquy on the future of agriculture.

I was always embarrassed when my father talked about the Shah. I knew that Americans just weren't interested in the guy, but my father seemed to think that all Americans were on the edge of their seats, wondering what modernization plans lay ahead for Iran. But a conversation in English with my father was a one-way street, with the listener wondering how many more miles till the next rest stop. My father's ignorance of body language did not help. To him, a glazed look, slumped posture, and open jaw were the American way of saying, "Go on, you fascinating foreigner!"

In Iran, the Shah's picture was on the front page of textbooks, in offices, in banks, and in schools, keeping him foremost in people's thoughts. No wall space had been overlooked for this decorating opportunity, although I'm sure that even Ms. Shirley Ruth would have found the "leader's face" theme a bit redundant and could have suggested something with a little more color, perhaps with tassels. And of course, all the photos were very serious. Although a smiling photo would have added much more to the ambiance of any bank, school, or government office, it would have taken away a certain dictatorial edge, and that would have been a real decorating faux pas.

Sitting next to my father on our brown, beige, and tangerine striped sofa, I was enduring the itchiness of my outfit, waiting for my chance to speak to the reporter. I had already chosen my topic.

June, the dear journalist, asked my brother Farshid what he thought of life in America. My brother gave a typically predictable answer about how much he liked wrestling, soccer, and karate. His answer was edited to read, "Farshid enjoys American school . . ."

Then June asked my mother her feelings on America. My mom delivered an incomprehensible collection of words that were written as "I haven't been homesick once since we came here and we feel the schools are marvelous." I understood June's predicament. To have directly quoted my mother's "So very good pee-pel so good at Veet-e-yerr" would not have worked. But anyone who had ever spoken to my mother would have known that the sentence attributed to her in the paper could not have happened. Her use of verbs, a trisyllabic adjective, a sentence that could be understood by an English-speaking person—all were dead giveaways that June had, let's just say, used her imagination. But this was okay, because June had a job to do and bills to pay.

I was still waiting for my turn to speak. I had decided to enlighten June on the difference in the level of expectation in Iranian and American schools. I was going to tell her that in Iran we had to stand up when a teacher entered the room, and how much homework we had and how no one ever dared speak back to the teacher and that even though I liked my teachers in America, I had actually learned a lot more in Iran.

As I sat with a smile plastered on my face, I thought about how much more interesting my comments were going to be than those of the rest of my family and I wondered what size came after fourteen Pretty Plus, since the waistband on my pants was definitely getting tight. Suddenly, June turned to my father and said, "And now a few questions about your daughter. How do you pronounce her name?"

I don't know what school of pseudojournalism June had bought her diploma from, but if I understood correctly, she was going to be asking my father about *me,* not *me* about *me.* My father, happy and willing to steal the limelight from his own kin, told June how I hadn't spoken any English when I first arrived and how my mother had accompanied me to school for the first three days and then had been told by me to stay home. This, of course, was wrong. My mother had accompanied me for only *one* day before I asked her to stay home. I didn't want to contradict my father in front of June, plus I assumed I would eventually have a chance to speak a few words myself—but no. June then closed her writing tablet, thanked us, and moved out of the way so the photographer could take a few snapshots. I had been nothing more than a photo opportunity.

When the article was published, my parents were quite pleased with the photo, although years later my father did declare his three-inch sideburns rather dated and unattractive.

What irked me, besides not having been interviewed, was the last sentence. My parents had told June that my brothers would both be staying in America while the three of us were preparing to return to Iran, and that we hoped to be able to return to America someday. June wrote, "Until the day for making a decision arrives, it seems safe to assume the U.S. will have two unofficial members of the diplomatic corps serving in the Middle East." *Two* members, according to June—so who was she leaving out? Was I not an unofficial member of the diplomatic corps serving in the Middle East? Was I, who had not only learned English fluently but had also eaten Frosted Flakes, Chips Ahoy! cookies, and Hamburger Helper on a daily basis; watched enough TV to have earned the nickname "TV Guide"; and become an overweight, sedentary, polyester-clad American, not good enough for the diplomatic corps?

Dear June, perhaps you would like to have an interview with me now, but I'm sorry. I'm busy.

His and Hers

There are only a few things in life that cause sheer jubilation in my father, and clearance sales are one of them. When I was sixteen, my father came home one day and breathlessly announced that the nearby engineering corporation was selling all its old furniture. "Nothing over seventy-nine dollars!" he kept repeating, trying to put a lid on his excitement.

The following Saturday, my father and I woke up bright and early. Armed with the checkbook, we set out for the bargain hunt. We decided to take both cars. At the time, my father drove a Buick LeSabre, a fancy French word meaning "OPEC thanks you." Our behemoth was, as described by the dealer, a "two-toned mulberry." Farshid referred to it as "Dad's purple car," a term that greatly disturbed my father, which in turn guaranteed its constant repetition by the aforementioned brother. The dealer had knocked off a few hundred dollars to try to get the ugly-mobile off his hands, and even though my mother had said, "Kazem, it's *really* ugly," the car was now ours. It wasn't just the color. Its roof was not only a deeper shade of the mulberry/purple/magenta theme, but was made of leatherette, giving our car the vehicular equivalent of a cheap toupee. The good thing about our car, as my father repeatedly reminded us, was that it was very easy to spot in a parking lot. This could have been just as easily achieved by sticking a toilet plunger on the roof of any car.

For our foray into bargaindom, I was to drive the silver Chevette, a car with a history that could fill several tomes. We had purchased the Chevette the year before, when my mother finally decided to learn to drive. She used to drive in Abadan, a town where, during commuting hours, she may have had to share the road with up to five cars. She had never driven in Tehran and had adamantly refused even to try to drive in America. Of course, driving in America is totally different from driving in Iran since, here, traffic rules have to be somewhat obeyed. In Iran, stop signs and red lights are merely decorative. In fact, stopping at a stop sign would probably cause a rear-end collision.

When my mother obtained her California driver's license, she announced that she would not drive at night, on freeways, or on any road with too many cars, a term not clearly defined by her but understood by the rest of us as "You're still going to have to drive me places." Due to my mother's limited automobile needs, my father decided to buy her a Chevette, a car that in automobile evolution stands proudly one rung above the golf cart. He purchased the bare-bones model, the one that came with a steering wheel, four tires, seats, a rearview mirror, and an AM radio. This was fine for my mother, but for me, someone whose friends were receiving convertibles for their Sweet Sixteen birthdays, the Chevette was no social coup. Worse yet, the only radio station that came in clearly specialized in easy-listening tunes, in particular the vast repertoire of Perry Como, a singing legend whom I now much appreciate. But back in the eighties, I would have preferred to be singing "Hungry Like the Wolf" with Duran Duran.

The musical limitations of the Chevette were minor compared with its other problem—acceleration. This was a vehicle that went from zero to fifty-five in nine and a half minutes. Merging on the freeway was an ulcer in the making. As I pressed on the accelerator, sweating and praying, other drivers made rude gestures, honked, or mouthed four-letter words as they passed me. Not even Mr. Como's gentle voice reminding me of "Bali Ha'i" could help me. "It's not a *Corvette!*" I wanted to scream. If I had a hammer, I could've given Mr. Como a whole other verse. A decade later, "road rage" was born in Southern California and added to the American lexicon. I was a pioneer in that movement.

Not only did my mother and I learn to drive using the Chevette, so did two dozen visiting relatives from Iran. Anytime anyone remotely related to me needed to learn how to drive, they borrowed the Chevette. Aside from the fact that no one else was willing to lend student drivers a car, we owned the cheapest car, the one with presumably the most inexpensive replacement parts, should the need arise. Miraculously, the need never arose. Not only did everyone in my family pass his driver's test, but the accident-free Chevette served us well for ten years. My father eventually replaced it out of vanity, claiming that it stood out in a bad way among all the Mercedes in the neighborhood.

My father and I arrived at the furniture sale and were

greeted by a sea of desks, cabinets, chairs, and bookcases covering the entire parking lot. With our hearts pounding, we selected a huge desk (seventy-nine dollars), a chair (thirty-nine dollars), and a file cabinet (nineteen dollars). Then brilliance struck. My father said, "These desks are so cheap. Let's buy two."

"Great idea!" I chimed in, proving that cerebral limitations are often genetic.

By then, all the other seventy-nine-dollar desks were gone, so we settled for a slightly smaller fifty-nine-dollar model. We paid, and that's when our dilemma crystallized. We were expected to transport our two desks, two chairs, and a file cabinet ourselves. We looked around and noticed the other customers hoisting their purchases onto their trucks and U-Hauls. My father opened the trunk of the LeSabre and announced, "I think it'll work." Even though the trunk was the size of an eight-person Jacuzzi, the seventy-nine-dollar desk was the size of a sixteen-person Jacuzzi. My father began trying to lift the desk into the car when two benevolent souls came to his aid. "I don't think this is gonna fit," one of them surmised. "It'll fit," my father said. "Just help me lift it in here." The two men helped lift the desk and placed it on its side in the trunk. It stuck out like an iceberg. The men offered to help my father tie it down. Of course my father had not brought any rope. "I'll just drive slowly," he said. Then, like preparing a Thanksgiving turkey, my father stuffed the chairs and the file cabinet inside the car and moved on to the Chevette. He opened the hatchback and shoved in the other desk, which didn't fit, either, but my father didn't seem to notice. "Just drive slowly," he said.

If life came with background music, the *Jaws* theme would have started then.

We set out driving twenty miles per hour in the forty-five-mile-per-hour zone. I was following my father when a police car came between us. The officer tailed my father quietly for a few miles. Suddenly my father pulled to the side of the road, even though the officer had not flashed his lights or used his siren. I pulled to the side and got out of the Chevette. I could see my father looking very nervous. As the officer heard my footsteps, he turned around quickly and yelled, "Who are you?"

"I'm his daughter," I replied. "I just thought he might need some help with his English," I added.

In another era, this officer could have made his living in a circus sideshow. An obvious devotee of bodybuilding, this man was solid. As I stared into the eyes of this neckless wonder, it appeared that where the instructions on the steroid powder had said "one teaspoon," this man had used a cup.

"Why did you stop?" he yelled at my father.

My father nervously tried to explain that he had stopped because he wanted to make sure his load was safe.

"You stopped, so I'm giving you a ticket," the cop announced.

"But he didn't do anything," I said. "He stopped on his own accord. I bet there are probably crimes being committed right now, and you're ticketing people for stopping?"

"Who asked you to speak?" the cop yelled at me.

He reminded me of when I was a little girl in Abadan and every so often I would find a fly with damaged wings. I would kneel on the floor, observing it closely, knowing that it was scared of me but had no power to get away. Now we were that fly.

"Where's your car?" the cop asked me.

I pointed to the Chevette.

"You're getting a ticket, too," he said smugly.

"You are the most irresponsible policeman . . ." I told him. That's when my father told me to be quiet, in Persian.

The policeman, who was clearly uncomfortable hearing us speak a foreign language, looked at me and said, "Did you know I can give you a ticket for slandering a police officer?"

I shut up.

After he wrote both of us tickets for having unsafe loads, he told us that we were not allowed to drive with these goods and that if we attempted to do so, he would issue us a second set of tickets.

We stood on the side of the road pondering our predicament. My dad asked me if I knew anyone who owned a truck. That was like asking me if I knew anybody in Newport Beach who was out of shape. Newport Beach is not an area known for diversity, corporal, vehicular, or otherwise. Diversity was limited to the various German carmakers represented in any given parking lot.

I couldn't think of anyone with a truck, but I did recall that one of our neighbors owned a van. Since we were nowhere near a phone, my father and I unloaded the fifty-nine-dollar desk out of the Chevette and I drove off to try to find Susan, our van-owning neighbor.

Susan, God bless her, happened to be home, and agreed to help us out. She drove back and forth several times, helping us bring our purchases home. My older brothers, Farid and Farshid, helped unload the goods into the hallway of our condo.

The furniture had looked much more desirable in the parking lot. Without the hordes of other shoppers milling around, it now looked cumbersome and ugly. Granted, all the pieces were in great condition, except of course for the damage they had incurred in our attempts to bring them home. Their fine condition spoke volumes about the engineers who had once used them. There were no initials carved in the chairs, no gum underneath the desks, and no profane doodles anywhere.

"This is really ugly," my mother declared of one of the desks.

"It's huge and ugly," Farid added.

"You two should never be trusted to make any type of decision," Farshid declared.

And we hadn't even told them about the tickets.

My father, visibly upset yet managing to ignore all the comments, asked my brothers to help him carry the first of the desks upstairs. This is when they ran into a problem that made our other problems appear minor. The desk was wider than our staircase.

Meanwhile, my mother was doing her best imitation of a radio station, KNAG.

"This is *the* ugliest stuff ever."

"What were you thinking?"

"Maybe if you go back now, you can return it."

My father, who even in the face of a glaring mistake will insist that he is right, told my brothers that if they carried the desk on its side, it would fit. As he shared his brilliant plan, I could see the vein throbbing in his neck, a sign that we were only moments away from a volcanic outburst.

As my brothers and father were attempting to turn the desk on its side, my mother reminded my father of the time he had hurt his back washing his feet in the shower while standing up, and how the doctor had told him that he should not lift heavy things. Before she could finish her soliloquy, the volcano formerly known as my father erupted.

My mother was quite upset that her helpful remarks were not appreciated. Normally, she would have gone and sulked somewhere, but not today. There had not been this much action on our staircase since the annoying son of one of our distant relatives got his head stuck between the stairway railings.

Even on its side, the desk barely fit the staircase. As my brothers started to climb the stairs, my mother yelled, "Stop! You're scraping the wall!"

"It doesn't matter," my father said. "Keep going."

My brothers managed to carry the desk all the way up the stairs, leaving a deep gash along the entire wall. Hundreds of years from now, archaeologists will study the ancient wall and try to decipher the meaning of the hieroglyphic line. After years of research, one of the scientists will announce, "Desk too big."

It came as no surprise that the desk did not fit in the doorway of my bedroom, but having carried the monster upstairs, my brothers were not about to carry it back down. With my father giving orders to my brothers to "just keep going," interspersed with orders to my mother to "just keep quiet," my brothers managed to force the desk into my tiny room, but not before breaking the molding around my door.

My once-tiny room all but disappeared. It was now a desk.

My father surveyed the scene and announced, "It looks great!" He ran down the stairs and brought up one of the swivel chairs. "Sit behind your new desk!" he ordered me, trying to conceal the obvious: we had bought a big, ugly desk that was more appropriate for a coroner performing autopsies than for a sixteen-year-old doing math homework.

My brothers then carried the other pieces upstairs and placed everything in their old room, which not surprisingly already had a desk, chair, and bookcase in it. Their old room now looked like an office furniture showroom. All that was missing was a sign declaring, "Visa and MasterCard Accepted!"

Like the curse that befell those who disturbed Tutankhamen's tomb, the furniture continued to bring misery to my parents' condo. The scraped walls, the gashed doorways, the useless furniture that took up half of our living space, the $220 spent on traffic tickets—these were often starting points for conversations that ended with at least one person sulking.

Once I graduated from high school, my parents decided to get rid of the desks, chairs, and bookcase. But getting rid of a Pinto would have been easier.

My parents placed an ad in the paper. This resulted in a long parade of people, usually accompanied by screaming toddlers tracking dirt into our house, looking at the furniture, smiling, and leaving. This was always followed by an argument during which my mother would re-create that fateful shopping day and ending with my father watching television with the volume set on high.

After their paid ad expired, my parents decided to simply give away the furniture. They asked several of the gardeners who worked in their condo complex if they were interested. The gardeners were willing to come into the condo and look around, but none wanted the furniture. These were people earning minimum wage who labored all day and *they did not want the furniture for free*. This was a bad omen.

My parents began calling charitable organizations, all of which were interested only until being told of the approximate weight and second-floor location of the goods. Then they weren't interested.

Finally, my father called a handyman and offered him a

hundred dollars to remove the furniture. The handyman agreed.

One hundred dollars later, the furniture was history, except of course for the damage it had left on our walls and doorways. Erasing that memory took a few more years and a remodel, courtesy of my brother Farshid.

Without the physical evidence of the fiasco, my father has taken it upon himself to create his own version of the story, a sentimental tale involving father-daughter driving tickets. "It's not a story I care to remember," I tell him. "Plus," I remind him, "do you know how much that bargain furniture ended up costing us?"

That's when he turns on the TV, volume high.

The Jester and I

Most immigrants agree that at some point, we become permanent foreigners, belonging neither here nor there. Many tomes have been written trying to describe this feeling of floating between worlds but never fully landing. Artists, using every known medium from words to film to Popsicle sticks, have attempted to encapsulate the struggle of trying to hang on to the solid ground of our mother culture and realizing that we are merely in a pond balancing on a lily pad with a big kid about to belly-flop right in. If and when we fall into this pond, will we be singularly American or will we hyphenate? Can we hold on to anything or does our past just end up at the bottom of the pond, waiting to be discovered by future generations? At what point must we listen to the music of Kevin Federline?

I do not have the answers to any of these questions. All I know is that this feeling of being on the outside has shaped me into the perfect party guest. A roomful of strangers? No problem. A roomful of strangers who don't speak the same language? No problem. A roomful of strangers who have never tried sushi but who claim to hate it? A challenge, but I could do it.

The one and only time I felt like a complete foreigner was in college. Observing the behavior of college freshmen made me wonder if I belonged not just to the same culture but to the same species. Sure, we shared certain characteristics—backpacks full of textbooks, opposable thumbs—but the similarities ended there.

A big slice of college life happens after dark. That's a problem. I do not like to stay up really late, or even somewhat late, hence the magnetic nickname "Grandma" bestowed on me by my brother. I never saw *Saturday Night Live* until I had to nurse babies. I have always been much fonder of early mornings than late nights. Paris, Tehran, Idaho, or Berkeley at 6:00 AM is magical. At midnight, it's the same cast of characters, the same smells, the same endearing voices floating in the distance: "Back off, jerk, before I call the cops." It's fine with me that most people don't like early mornings. That's part of the magic, but apparently not so in college. Asking someone if they want to go for a walk before an 8:00 AM class is downright freakish, I discovered, one level more freakish even than signing up for an 8:00 AM class.

If there is something worth staying up for, I will. But that was the other problem. Almost all evening activities revolved around binge drinking. The common belief was that drinking made people more fun-loving. But the truth was that those people who needed to drink to be "fun-loving" were equally boring when they were drunk; they just didn't remember it.

Needless to say, I was very disappointed in college social

life. I discovered that my idea of fun—dinner at an ethnic restaurant, a foreign movie, and discussion afterward about minutiae—did not match the collegiate definition of "good times." For a majority of my fellow students, fun began with the magic words "We got a keg!"

My not drinking had nothing to do with my being Muslim or Iranian. When I was in high school, my father said that if I ever wanted to try alcohol, I could, but only at home. Of course there was never a drop of alcohol in my parents' house, but my father offered to buy whatever I wanted to try. This pretty much ruined any enjoyment I would have had in sneaking alcohol, the sneaking part being the magnetic component.

After spending my freshman and sophomore years trying to find people who shared my idea of fun, I pretty much gave up, but I did not go gently into that good night. If there was a group that sounded remotely interesting, I gave it a try. Since I lived off campus, I did not have the benefit of meeting people in the dorm. For my first attempt at finding my niche, I joined a church social group, thinking they didn't drink and might be fun. They probably would have been fun if there had been more than six of them and if I had not mentioned that I was Muslim. But I was right about one thing: they didn't drink.

Next I joined a group of volunteers who practiced English with foreigners. I met a lot of people who didn't speak English.

Then came a running group, which I quit in a record-breaking two weeks. The final straw was jogging with them through the hills of Berkeley and watching them become small dots in the distance, until they lost me. These people were not into jogging together and mingling. They just ran, fast.

Then came a group whose job was to promote team spirit at football games. I was really, really desperate since there was nothing about this group or its goals that interested me, not to mention that the only two things I know about football is that I don't like it and the game takes too long. I still cannot remember what prompted me to join this group, except for the sheer desire to belong to a group. But after three weeks, I quit. It was like a Hollywood marriage.

Then came the paying job of doing advertising for an aerobics studio. That job involved me, a staple gun, and telephone poles. No friends found there. Finally, I became a volunteer usher at the local performing arts center. This job came with the greatest perk ever—admission to all shows. Most of the other volunteers were adults and senior citizens who lived in Berkeley, so no bonding there. But in exchange for walking around with a flashlight and showing theatergoers where row K was, I was allowed to attend performances by world-class musicians and dancers. I saw dancers from Harlem, Taiwan, India, and Russia. I attended performances of Taiko Drummers, pianists, and artists I never knew existed, such as throat singers. I saw Merce Cunningham, Martha Graham, and the Peking Acrobats, a virtual all-you-can-soak-in buffet of culture, and all for free.

As much as I loved this new window in my life, I still yearned to meet someone my age, someone who shared my interests. I had made a few friends during my summer job as an orientation counselor, but once school started, everyone went back to his own routine. There was nothing in mainstream college for me.

To me, nothing symbolized mainstream Americans in college more than the Greek system. Every day, on my way to class, I walked past the rows of fraternity houses, in their permanent post-party state. At Berkeley, the fraternity houses are enormous, exquisite homes, most of which were originally built for professors. Today they are living proof why groups of men in their late teens and early twenties should never live together. Suppressing the urge to renovate, decorate, and landscape each and every one of their houses, I was nonetheless amused by the frat boys' endless quest to attract females, preferably scantily clad ones. Every hunter needs bait, and every weekend constituted a different theme party. There was the beach party (bikini tops, shorts), the luau (bikini tops, shorts, leis), the Mardi Gras (bikini tops, shorts, beads), and the fiesta (see "beach party").

I loved the idea of the parties, the themes, and the socializing, but the allure of a houseful of drunken men eluded me. I wanted conversation, or at least evidence of the possibility of conversation.

My junior year, I moved into Berkeley's International House, a residence for six hundred, comprising half American students, half foreign. It is the kind of place where one often sees an Israeli, a Palestinian, an Italian, and a student from Nebraska eating dinner together and discussing politics, soccer, and Bollywood. If every world leader could spend one year living at an International House, there would be far fewer wars. Of that, I am absolutely certain.

My reasons for moving into International House were far less noble. My cousin Mehrdad had lived there in the seventies and always said it was the most enjoyable year of his college life. He had shown me photos of him sitting on his bed, with long, unattractive sideburns, strumming his guitar surrounded by Anka, Lars, Sophronius, and Maria, all looking like they were having the best time of their lives. I always considered my cousin Mehrdad a fun-loving guy, but on my scale of "fun" relatives, I put myself higher. I figured if he had such a great time, I would have an even better time.

Because most foreign students who come to study in America are males, Berkeley's International House tends to have a shortage of female residents. The year I applied to be a resident, the shortage of female residents had reached its peak with a male-to-female ratio of nine to one. One need not be an accounting major to know that those are good numbers. For someone with a nonexistent dating history, and the self-esteem that goes with it, those numbers were God's way of telling me, "Do not worry, my little lamb. All shall be fixed."

When I moved in, my roommate, Debbie from Delaware, had not yet arrived. Anticipating her arrival, I bit my nails to the nubbins. Our room, with its bunk bed, two tiny desks, and one dresser, required harmony. I just didn't know if Debbie from Delaware and Firoozeh from Abadan would work.

Debbie turned out to be a premed major with a great sense of humor. I liked her right away, so much so that I told her that her chances of reaching her medical goals would be increased if she changed her name to Debra. Not only is Dr. Debra a bona fide doctor today, but she also teaches at a prestigious university. I take full credit, having saved her from her certain future as Debbie from Delaware, Director of Cheerleading Camp.

During my first week at International House, I discovered that one couldn't spit without hitting someone interesting and smart. Foreign countries do not send their dumbest abroad (although that is a policy with potential benefits). Debra and I met people from all over, all of whom knew something about Iran but nothing about Delaware. "Where *is* Delaware?" spoken in a multitude of accents began every conversation.

Debra was a worthy ambassador for her state. "Delaware was the first state to ratify the Constitution," she'd always say. "The state motto is 'Liberty and Independence,'" she would add. But no matter how many people Debra enlightened, the masses remained oblivious to the significance or location of Delaware. This, of course, brought me much satisfaction, since for the first time since living in America I was not the one having to explain my birthplace.

Two weeks after I moved in, I was eating lunch in the cafeteria with a group of fellow residents. Among them was Walter, an American I later renamed Noorallah (Light of God) due to his affinity for Middle Easterners. Walter noticed another International House student eating lunch by himself and, in typical I-House fashion, invited him to join us. There was only one empty seat and it was next to me.

After François from France introduced himself, I told him that I had just finished a course on contemporary French writers and asked him if he was familiar with the topic. "Yes," he said, rather enthusiastically. "So, which authors are you familiar with?" I asked. He stared at me with a blank look and said, "Uh . . . uh . . . ."

Then, in an attempt to overcompensate, he started telling me about a short story written by Boris Vian that he had particularly liked, giving too much detail, a sure sign that this was the only story he had ever read. I figured François was a typical engineering major who had once read a piece of fiction in the dentist's office. I finished my lunch and left.

The next evening, during coffee hour, I once again ran into François, who did his best to engage me in conversation. We talked a bit, but then I decided that I did not want to spend my entire evening talking to just one person, since, according to my calculations, eight other males awaited me. I ended the conversation rather ungraciously. Later, François once again found me and made an attempt at conversation, and once again I found an excuse to leave quickly.

The next day, I felt really bad. As someone who understood how hard it was to meet people at a huge university, I was ashamed that I had acted so unlike myself. I decided to apologize to François by leaving him a note and inviting him out for coffee, but I wanted to make sure he knew it wasn't a date. After writing several versions of my note, I read the final one to Debra, who assured me it gave the right friendly vibe and nothing more. I told her that I would also bring up the topic of Delaware, which would make it clear that it wasn't a date, since with the exception of the governor of Delaware, no one talks about Delaware on a date. Debra agreed.

I left the note on François's door and waited for him to call. It was Thursday.

He didn't call on Friday. On Saturday morning, I told Debra, "He thought it was a date, and now he's snubbing me." On Saturday, I told Debra, "I hate him." Debra agreed to hate him with me. On Sunday, I told her, "I have to move out of International House now."

Late Sunday night, François called to say that he had been out of town and hadn't received my note. He said he would love to go out for coffee.

The following evening, after dinner, we went to Café Roma, an outdoor café a block from the dorm. We talked and talked. Next thing I knew, it was almost midnight. François walked me back to my room, hugged me good night, and told me that he couldn't remember the last time he had enjoyed talking to someone so much. He also invited me for coffee the following night.

The following evening, we talked and talked. This guy was the best storyteller I had ever met and a real gentleman to boot. And he was cute.

The next night, he invited me to his room to show me his

books. I'd seen enough episodes of *The Love Boat* to know what was coming my way. So I went to his room and, wouldn't you know it, he showed me his books. He had more books than I could imagine anybody lugging from France—paperbacks, entire series in hardcover, even big coffee-table books. He had books on Hiroshige, Hafez, and Hemingway, not to mention an entire shelf of contemporary French writers. I asked him why he couldn't name any contemporary authors the first time we met, since he clearly had read dozens of them. "It's a long story," he said. "I didn't get housing when I came from France so I was advised to join a fraternity, which would guarantee me a room near campus. It's a crazy place, these American fraternities," he said. I nodded. He continued, "Every weekend, everyone gets drunk. There are no conversations, so when you asked me about contemporary writers, I was so happy at the idea of having an intelligent conversation, that my mind went blank. So anytime you want to go out for coffee and talk, I am available."

We sat in his tiny room as he told me about his family and his life in France and Greece. He described Platania, where he spent every summer of his life. He described the foods he ate there and the difference in the sea in the morning and night.

I knew I had found someone special, someone with depth and soul.

As I was sharing a personal story about my past, François smiled, looked at me, and said, "You know something? You've quite a chest there."

I was stunned. It was such an out-of-place comment, so *creepy*.

Noticing my expression, François quickly added, "I mean that as a compliment! I *really* like this about you."

I wasn't quite sure what to say. All of a sudden, the room

seemed really small and the books seemed like bait—perhaps more intelligent bait than a Free Margaritas for All the Ladies sign, but bait nonetheless. (At least the signs were more honest.)

"Maybe you have more in common with your fraternity brothers than you realize," I told him.

He feigned surprise. "Why do you say that?"

"When you said you were happy to have found someone to talk to, I guess what you meant is you are happy to have found someone with *breasts,*" I said, emphasizing the word "breasts" to indicate that I had seen right through his little gentleman act. "Next time you lure a girl, I mean *breasts,* to your room, you might try some subtlety, Mr. Senseeteev Literature Man."

Even though François had no accent, I faked a French accent because it just seemed like the right thing to do.

He looked all flustered. "I don't understand," he said. "All I said was 'You're quite a jester.'"

"Oh," I said.

There was a long, awkward pause.

"You shouldn't use the word 'jester,'" I told him. "It's confusing. It is technically a word, but nobody uses it in America."

François looked perplexed.

"It's like 'nosegay,'" I explained. "No one uses that word, either. It would only lead to confusion, maybe a fight."

François looked alarmed, so I continued.

"'Codpiece,' 'hurdy-gurdy.'" I could have gone on and on. But instead, François leaned over in that cramped, book-filled room and kissed me. Perhaps it was his way of changing the conversation.

He has not used the word "jester" since.

A Moveable Feast

People always ask me how I remember the details of my past. "Did you keep a journal your whole life?" "Do you make things up?"

Truth is, I have a memory for certain things and not for others. For me, watching any movie is like watching it for the first time, every time. I cannot remember plots, character names, or pretty much any other detail that may prove that I actually saw the movie. I can, however, recall, in perfect detail, the meal I had prior to seeing the movie.

My keys are another story. Every day, I spend a good part of my life looking for my key chain. I even bought a key hanger at a street fair and hung it by my front door, but that is the last place I look. The places my keys have actually turned up include in the refrigerator, the dirty laundry, and the pocket of whatever I was wearing the day before, that jacket that I didn't remember wearing.

The one thing, however, that I never, ever forget is a face.

When I was seventeen, I spent a long, lonely summer in Paris. The French family I was staying with decided to spend the summer in the country, *sans moi*. I was left in the apartment in Paris. Faced with more free time than I knew what to do with, I bought a guidebook and set out to attempt to see every museum in Paris. The problem is, going to museums is like riding a seesaw: fifteen minutes alone and you realize something is missing. Half the fun of going to museums is discussing the artwork.

"How do they know they didn't hang that one upside down?"

"I could do that."

After several weeks of viewing mummies, Impressionists, Fauvists, Cubists, bronzes, relics of the Ming dynasty, restored mansions, and Edith Piaf's stuffed cat, I wanted to see something outside of Paris. I read a few more guidebooks and decided to buy a bus ticket to see Mont St. Michel, a place that God must have created with the help of Alfred Hitchcock and Edgar Allan Poe. Mont St. Michel, a quasi-island in Normandy, is the site of a magnificent chapel built in the tenth century. During low tide, visitors can walk to the site, but during high tide, Mont St. Michel becomes an island. The tide comes in at one meter per second, or as Victor Hugo described it, *"à la vitesse d'un cheval au galop,"* which sounds so nice in French and not so bad in English, either, "as swiftly as a galloping horse." But that's not all! The tide comes with thick fog, creating constantly shifting quicksand. In other words, *sayonara*. I had read many descriptions of poor souls getting lost and finding themselves caught, not just in the rushing tide but in the troika of tide, fog, and quicksand. The only thing that could possibly make this scenario any more frightening would be the addition of dragons. I had to see this place.

A couple of days later, I found myself on a bus filled with camera-toting tourists, all of us ready for the four-hour drive. I found an empty seat, and a few minutes later a young couple sat in front of me. Immediately, they formed what I can best describe from my Girl Scout handbook as a sailor's knot. His knee on her knee, her knee on his knee, her arms twisted around him, his arms wrapped around her face. A few seconds later, she started nibbling on his earlobe; he kissed her neck. We were barely out of the parking lot. She licked his cheek; he chewed on her ear cartilage. They were either in love or very hungry.

I didn't want to stare at them and yet they were seated directly in front of me and there were no other empty seats on the bus. I looked out the window, then back at The Knot. Now they had seemingly velcroed the top of their foreheads together as they stared at each other, in what I imagined must have been a somewhat blurry gaze at that distance. Their love was in focus even if their eyes were starting to cross. Then the nibbling started again, and I once more gazed out my window, pretending to be interested in the patterns in French traffic.

This went on for the duration of the ride. They stopped only when we stopped at a sandwich shop for lunch. I'm not even sure they took a break during lunch; I just made sure I was nowhere near them.

When we arrived at Mont St. Michel, we all went our separate ways.

Having read Henry James's description of Mont St. Michel, and having seen it in the Bayeaux Tapestry during one of my many museum excursions, I was impressed. The only downside was the herds of tourists. There were no tourists in Henry James's descriptions, just Henry and his deep thoughts. Now there were gift shops and people from all over the world who, granted, had as much right to be there as I did. I would have preferred the company of just Henry James.

I returned to Paris that night, spent a couple more weeks visiting museums, then packed my bags and returned to Newport Beach. As soon as I saw my parents at the airport, I confessed to them that I had actually been alone for the summer.

"But what about the letters you wrote us describing the family and your host mom's great cooking?" they asked. "I made it up," I told them. They were not amused. I told them that had they known the truth, I would have had to come home, thus guaranteeing a depressing summer. This way, I had a lonely and somewhat depressing summer but learned a foreign language along the way. "Plus," I continued, "being depressed in Paris is so noble, so normal. It's the perky ones that worry the French. I fit right in."

With the summer behind me, I was now a senior in high school and had to apply to colleges. My father decided that I should attend UC Berkeley. "Best deal in the country!" he kept saying. "Nobel laureates everywhere!"

My father was right about that. I did attend several large lectures given by Nobel laureates. Oddly enough, they all started out with the same joke: "The best part of winning the Nobel Prize was receiving my own parking space at UC Berkeley."

During my junior year, while walking in Sproul Plaza, the

main entrance to the university, a young woman walking in front of me turned to speak to her companion. When I saw her profile, I knew I had seen that face before. I just could not remember where.

These kinds of things keep me up at night. Whenever I see someone I think I know, I have to figure out how I know him. This has at times led to embarrassing circumstances, such as when I mistook a woman in the grocery store for a college classmate when it turned out I "knew" her because she was a world-renowned athlete. If curiosity killed the cat, my days are certainly numbered.

A week later, while walking in Sproul Plaza, I saw the same woman again. This time, I caught up with her, tapped her on the shoulder, and told her that I knew her from somewhere but couldn't remember where. She looked at me and said she didn't know me.

"I know I know you," I said.

"I don't think so," she said.

This being Berkeley, she probably thought I was recruiting her for something. This was also the period when I wore only black.

All of a sudden, I remembered. "Were you by any chance in Paris in the summer of 1982?" I asked. She hesitated and said yes.

I continued: "Did you take a bus to Mont St. Michel with your boyfriend?"

She paused for a moment, and gazed at me with a look that combined both fear and bewilderment. "Yes," she said again, even more hesitantly.

"I was sitting behind you!" I declared enthusiastically.

She was rather stunned. "I can't believe you remember me," she said.

"I remember your boyfriend, too," I added. I immediately regretted saying that, but it was too late. But then I thought, I've gone too far, why not go farther. "Is he still your boyfriend?" I asked. I was interested for a couple of reasons. The first being nosiness and the second being nosiness.

"Yes. As a matter of fact, he is coming to visit me next week. He's at graduate school at Brown," she added.

I made a mental note *not* to sit behind them.

Oddly enough, The Nibbler and I ended up becoming friends. She was a teacher's assistant in the French department at Berkeley studying for her Ph.D. in French history. She told me that her trip to Mont St. Michel had been part of her studies, a valid reason for anyone to major in the humanities.

Since I was an undergrad and she a graduate student, people always asked us how we knew each other. "It's a long story involving a monastery and an earlobe," I always replied.

Me and Mylanta

My first year in college, I managed to get an ulcer. This was not hard to do since I spent my days and nights worrying.

A few years before I entered college, the Iranian Revolution had left my father with almost nothing, including no job. My going away to college was a huge financial burden, one that had been alleviated somewhat with scholarships. But any cash-strapped student will agree that the expenses in college are endless. Textbooks cost as much as Italian shoes, tickets to fly home once in a while don't come cheap, and there's always food.

To add to my worries, there was my mother. My poor mother did not want me to go away to college. I was the first woman on either side of my family to leave home for an undergraduate education, and this did not sit well with her. "Live at home and go to UC Irvine," she kept repeating. "We'll buy you a car," she always added, upping the ante.

Unfortunately for her, I had chosen to attend UC Berkeley, a school that has a rather unfair reputation as the vortex of all things strange. The thousands of "normal" students who attend UC Berkeley seem to be a well-kept secret. As soon as one odd duck is found—say, a nudist or someone who thinks paying taxes is illegal—the media has a field day, thus cementing the school's reputation as "Berserkley." When the Unabomber was caught, all the newspapers trumpeted the fact that he had taught at UC Berkeley. They barely mentioned that he had graduated from Harvard.

To strengthen the anti-Berkeley campaign, there was the friend of one of my father's co-workers from Abadan, whose nephew had attended UC Berkeley as a premed and who had switched to . . . art. This may seem like nothing to a Westerner, but to Iranian parents, a son majoring in art is a permanent bachelor who will be occupying the guest room, forever. According to my father's friend, this boy, nicknamed Dr. Koochooloo (Little Doc), had always enjoyed playing doctor with the neighborhood kids, and now he spent his days sculpting nude statues that, according to this co-worker, were not even good. Not to mention that the market for naked statues in my Muslim culture is right up there with the market for pork products.

My father was thrilled that I had been accepted to UC Berkeley. He could not wait to have another engineer in the family.

I had my own reasons for wanting to move away. As wonderful as it is to have a large extended family nearby, there are downsides. Not sure if your haircut is flattering? Don't worry. The relatives will tell you . . . the minute they see you.

"All I see now is your chins."

"Did you go to one of those discount salons?"

"It'll grow back, thank goodness."

I needed distance.

During our drive to Berkeley, none of us had much to say. My father tried to lighten the mood by reading the signs on the freeway and making really stupid jokes.

"Coalinga! What kind of name is that? Why don't they call their town Coca-Cola? It would be so much more popular!"

"Why are there so many signs for 'Anderson's Pea Soup'?"

"Hey, I'm going to open my own restaurant: Kazem's *Kaleh Pacheh*!"

Eight hours, dozens of bad jokes, and three Denny's meals later, we arrived in Berkeley. We drove straight to the apartment that we had rented sight unseen.

I was living off campus not by choice but by necessity. Berkeley in those days had a massive housing shortage, and assignments were based on a lottery. I did not get in the dorms my freshman year, which meant I either had to find a place off campus or pitch a tent.

The apartment was a typical one-bedroom college dwelling about fifteen minutes' walking distance from campus, right next door to the Bing Wong Laundromat. We carried my belongings to my apartment, ignoring the abandoned shopping cart and other telltale signs of a street person living in the apartment building's garage.

We piled my boxes in the apartment and went looking for a place to eat dinner. As the three of us walked down Telegraph Avenue, Berkeley's famous main street, my mother started to cry. Having spent the past eight years in Newport

Beach in a planned condominium community where flowers were replaced *before* they wilted, she was wholly unprepared for the certain je ne sais quoi of Telegraph Avenue. People with matted hair lay on the sidewalks, either asking for handouts or selling homemade bracelets, chunky clay mugs, and pipes. A tarot reader advertised his supposed skills on one corner. Another guy did brisk business selling Ronald "Raygun" T-shirts. The most "different" was the man wearing sandwich boards espousing conspiracy theories on everything from John Lennon's murder to the building of the pyramids.

The college brochure had described Telegraph Avenue as "lively." Perhaps describing it truthfully—"a freakish locale full of druggies sure to scare most parents"—would have diminished its charm. And then there was the smell, a mixture of patchouli, sweat, and a certain *odeur* later identified as pot.

We assumed these were all students, my future classmates, taking a break from their studies to warm up the sidewalks. Every few minutes, my mother broke the silence.

"Don't ever eat there."

"Or there."

"Don't ever talk to those people."

"Are we still in America?"

This was my first visit to Berkeley, and I hated it. But there was no turning back. I had no options but to feel really, really bad. And I did.

My parents left the next day. There were no teary goodbyes, just a shell-shocked perfunctory hug followed by my father's reminder: "Call us whenever you want. It doesn't matter if you wake us up."

"We won't be sleeping anyway," my mother added.

When they left, I stared at the avocado-green shag carpet and wondered how many species of insects had laid eggs in my apartment.

School started the following week. All my introductory freshman classes were huge. My chemistry class had seven hundred students. I met no one. I was not on a sports team, had no hobbies, and did not belong to any group. I did attend several social events at the local church, hoping to meet clean-cut types, but once they found out I was Muslim, they could barely contain themselves. Convinced I was a project sent from Above, they did their best to save me. But my soul was fine; I was just looking to be saved from boredom.

My lack of a social life meant that weekends were spent at the library, where I didn't study much. Truth be told, I spent my mental energies feeling sorry for myself. As I sat in the library cubicle reading the graffiti left by generations past, I thought about how much I had hated high school, even though it was supposed to have been the best years of my life. And now I was in college, which were definitely supposed to be the best years of life, and here I sat, on a Saturday night, sneaking a bag of chips in the library.

When I started to have severe pains in my stomach on an ongoing basis, I assumed I was dying. I accepted my self-diagnosis without much of a fight. It just seemed like a fitting end to my life. I hadn't gone to my high school prom. I had no idea what I wanted to do with my life. I had never learned how to use hair products correctly. I hated all my classes. I was wasting money on an education that somebody else would have appreciated much more.

I didn't bother going to the doctor. I spent hours every day imagining the reactions of various friends and family members to the news of my early demise. It filled the time that college students normally spend laughing and bonding with friends, living the best years of their lives.

It wasn't until I came home for a vacation that my parents took me to the doctor. They were shocked to discover that I had been feeling ill for months and had not bothered to tell anyone. They didn't realize that in my head, the full impact of my early demise could be attained only if it came as a total shock. No sneak previews of my death were allowed.

I was very disappointed to find out I had an ulcer. "Are you *sure* it's not fatal?" I asked the doctor. My entire fantasy life, or rather fantasy death, was blown away with a simple pill and a few chugs of Mylanta. I was very disappointed.

I returned to Berkeley with a somewhat better attitude and resigned myself to my boring life, a life that would never be made into a movie, except maybe one of those Ingmar Bergman types where nothing happens. I figured in life there were those who lived exciting lives, and then there was the audience. I had a permanent seat in the front row.

Through sheer will, I convinced myself that not having a social life had a positive consequence. Unlike other college girls, I did not have to spend hours in the shallow pursuit of "getting ready," since I had nowhere to go. My versatile wardrobe of navy blue sweat pants and tennis shoes took me from bed to class to library and back again. Better yet, the elastic waistband accommodated my daily diet of ninety-nine-cent pizza slices and bagels the size of my head.

I eventually decided to put my free time to good use and join the workforce. Like most unemployed people with no marketable skills, I wasn't about to settle for just any old job. I wanted one with little or no responsibility, high pay, and a stimulating work environment. No cog in a wheel for me. I wanted a job befitting my unique set of skills. And no matter how much money anyone dangled in my face, I would not compromise my principles.

I found a job stapling flyers to telephone poles and bulletin boards. This scintillating job allowed me to walk all over the city of Berkeley with a staple gun, defacing public property. The woman who had hired me was an aerobics teacher with a fledgling studio who wore leg warmers as a permanent accessory. She wanted her flyers everywhere, "as if a big bird pooped them all over town," she told me. She also instructed me "not to forget the trees." When I told her that stapling flyers to trees is probably illegal, not to mention damaging, she mentioned that by the time someone ripped down the flyer, she might snag one or two students. She also told me that walking around town would probably "be good for me."

Armed with my staple gun, I spent hours walking the streets of Berkeley. Problem was that there are only so many poles and bulletin boards, and each one already had three inches of flyers stapled to it, which I, frankly, enjoyed reading. Having grown up in Newport Beach among beautiful people driving beautiful cars, I had completely missed out on the culture of flyers. Reading them was like being invited into people's living rooms when they weren't home. I could make all sorts of assumptions and take my time doing so.

In order for me to actually do what I was hired to do, I had to cover up someone else's flyer, which, frankly, I didn't like doing. I spent hours reading other people's notices: landlords looking for students, students looking for teachers, teachers of pseudo-Indian relaxation techniques looking for stressed souls, and stressed souls looking for their lost pets. I wanted to help them all. I visualized happy endings for all their searches. But armed with my staple gun, I faced a moral dilemma. Whose flyer should I cover? Not the ones for lost pets. Those flyers inevitably included a photocopy of a cat that looked like every other cat I had ever seen. I was touched by the hope evident in the descriptions: "Has a black patch on his left side, a brown patch on his right leg and answers to 'Big Bubba.'" How a random person walking down the street was supposed to look at a skittish cat long enough to notice unique markings was beyond me, but nonetheless, I tried to learn some of the names just in case I ever ran into Big Bubba, Choo Choo, or Elvira.

I never covered up flyers for band members looking for musicians who were "serious and want to make awesome music together." Who was I to thwart someone's artistic dream? I admired the kind of person who would put up an ad for a drummer. At least he had a dream, however useless, impractical, and disappointing to his parents it might be. I always assumed that none of the people in the Band Member Wanted flyers were recent immigrants. No way would Arjun, Guan-Yin, or Omur ever dare tell their parents, "Actually, Mom and Dad, I've heard my calling, and it's a heavy metal band."

I did, however, cover signs for groups offering free vegetarian meals. I had heard about those so-called free meals. First, the nice people take your shoes so you can't leave. Then you have to sit through a very long lecture. Next thing you know, you're selling carnations at LAX. Lord knows how many lost souls I saved by redirecting them toward Jazzercise.

My stapling career ended when leg-warmer woman abruptly fired me, claiming she did not see enough flyers around town. She also had the nerve to tell me that I should consider taking her classes. I told her I knew a great place where she could get a free vegetarian meal.

After a string of menial jobs that made me understand why so many women aspire to marry rich men, I was hired as an orientation counselor. This job provided food and lodging for the summer, plus a salary. If that were not enough, the other counselors were interesting and smart, the types of people I had imagined meeting in college in the first place, but had not. I finally understood why people loved college.

One day close to the end of the summer, I woke up early to get ready. I went to the bathroom and when I went to flush, I froze. Even though I had not had a single symptom of my ulcer in over a year, I was bleeding. I remembered my doctor's words of warning: "If you ever see blood, that's bad." I started to panic. Everyone else was still sleeping.

I woke up my roommate. "I need you to take me to the hospital," I said.

She sat up in bed. "What's the matter?"

"I'm hemorrhaging," I told her, emphasizing the first syllable, making it clear that I was having a hard time saying the word since I was hemorrhaging. I don't know why I did not use the word "bleeding," but hemorrhaging felt more appropriate for the eventual Andrew Lloyd Webber musical of my life. "Don't cry for me, UC Berkeley," I would sing, arms outstretched, while the masses cried beneath my dorm balcony.

"Where are you bleeding?" my roommate asked.

"My intestines," I told her.

Truth was, I had no idea where the bleeding was, but I figured any organ that measures nine feet in length is a good bet.

I also noticed that I was speaking in a slower, raspier voice. I assumed this was my body's way of conserving my much-needed energy since life was literally being drained out of me.

My roommate wanted to call 911. I talked her out of it, still speaking in a raspy voice but also holding on to my stomach, holding everything in.

By the time she found one of the counselors who had a car, I was bent over, not out of pain but out of instinct. The other counselor also wanted to call 911, but I convinced him that I had enough time to make it to the hospital in his car. The hospital was five minutes away.

The three of us lumbered to the parking lot. My legs were feeling heavier and heavier, my breathing was more labored. But oddly enough, I had no pain whatsoever. I found it very odd that one could have internal bleeding and not feel a thing. It reminded me of an episode of *Oprah* where a crime victim who had been stabbed numerous times described how she could not feel a thing while she was being stabbed. I figured this was yet another example of the body shutting down in order to survive extreme pain.

I lay down in the backseat of the car. "Drive slowly," I said, still speaking in a raspy voice that was now getting softer and softer.

We arrived at the hospital after a few minutes and I was immediately taken to see the doctor. I assume the sight of me barely able to stand combined with the liberal usage of the words "hemorrhaging" and "internal bleeding" had allowed me, for the first time ever, not to have to wait endlessly to see a doctor. The counselors wanted to stay and hold my hand. My roommate was crying. I told them that because of the private nature of this exam, I would prefer that they leave. "Make sure someone takes over my freshmen group today,"

I told them, leaving them with the lasting impression of my sense of responsibility in the face of death.

As I lay on the examining table, I once again thought how odd it was that I had no pain whatsoever and yet I had seen with my own eyes that, well, there was red.

The doctor asked my medical history. I told her that my ulcer was bleeding. She asked me to describe the pain, which I could not since, frankly, there was none. She started the invasive physical exam, which requires no description.

Once it was over, she told me to lie still. Because of the urgent nature of my condition, the lab would process the results immediately.

Twenty minutes later she came back holding several sheets of paper.

"The results are in," she announced. "There was no trace of blood whatsoever."

"How could that be?" I asked. "My stools were red. It was quite clear. Maybe I should have saved them."

"Let me ask you something," she said. "Did you eat beets yesterday?"

"Most definitely not," I told her, feeling rather insulted that she was talking about a root vegetable as my life was being drained out of me, albeit in a painless way.

"What about beet juice?" she asked.

All of a sudden, I remembered. In my efforts to eat healthfully, I had purchased a carrot-beet-spinach juice combo the day before instead of my usual lamb burger with garlic fries.

"I can't remember," I said.

I got up and, no longer speaking in a raspy voice or holding my stomach, thanked her and picked up my clothes. Lacking the superpower strength to make myself completely invisible, I did what I always do when I should just be quiet—

I tried to be funny. "So I guess this is what they mean by 'the beet goes on'?"

She didn't laugh.

"If you ever eat asparagus," she said in an even more serious tone, "your urine will smell funny."

"I know," I told her. "That one everyone knows."

I changed and walked back to the dorms.

News of my grave condition had spread among my coworkers, and the remaining counselors were shocked to see me walk through the door. "Are you okay?" they asked.

"I'll be fine. I just have to take it easy for a couple of days," I told them.

"Of course," they said. "If there's anything we can do, just let us know."

"I will," I assured them. "I will."

'Twas the Fight
Before Christmas

The second year we were married, François decided to invite my parents for Christmas. "I want them to experience a French Christmas meal," he said, displaying the enthusiasm he reserves for elaborate menus.

My parents were more than happy. My father called the next day to give us their flight information. "We arrive at noon on December twenty-fifth," he said, "at Oakland Airport."

"That's the wrong airport!" I said.

"The airport near you guys was too expensive," he explained.

"They're arriving *when*!?" Francois asked, rather incredulously. "And why are they arriving at the wrong airport? Tell them to change their flight."

I called my father. "We can't change the flight," he said. "It's one of those special fares. We just won't come."

"No, of course not! We'll pick you up. No problem," I said.

François reluctantly agreed to change his Christmas lunch to a Christmas dinner. He also agreed to pick up my parents, since my father told him that I would probably get lost and they felt much more comfortable if he came.

"Your family is very difficult," François said.

"But they love you," I reminded him.

For the next three weeks, all our conversations centered around The Menu.

"Would your parents like carpaccio?"

"No."

"Would they try quail eggs?"

"No."

"Bone marrow on toast?"

"Dad, yes. Mom, definitely no."

My parents arrived on December 25 in jovial moods. This would be their first Christmas meal with somebody who actually celebrated Christmas, and they came laden with gifts. François put the gifts aside to be opened after dinner.

"Open them now!" my parents insisted, shoving their mismatched luggage behind the Christmas tree.

Many of my relatives had sent a gift or a card, each with my husband's name spelled differently, none correctly. François was nonetheless touched by the sentiment behind the misspellings. The cards were charming, in a nontraditional way. "Merry Christmas to Franseos! Many happy days and healthy!"

My parents always buy wrapping paper on sale, paying attention only to the pretty colors. As François held his stack of gifts, all emblazoned with "Happy Birthday!" and "Congratulations, Graduate!" he looked a bit puzzled. A steep learning curve lay ahead of him.

The first, second, and third gifts were tricolor sweaters
with the zigzaggy pattern so popular with infomercial sales-
men, men who wear bracelets, and my male relatives. After
that came the bottle of Paco Rabanne, a couple of ties, and a
pack of Calvin Klein underwear from my mother. My father
also gave us a Christmas ornament that read, "I Love Pugs!"
which he had found on the luggage carousel.

We also received packets of saffron, a bag of dried limes
for Persian stews, and my favorite snack, tamarind paste.

Once we opened what we thought were all the gifts, my
mother announced, "Von more for Fransva! Fransva, I make
you carrot jam vit pistachio. I know you like!"

She went into the living room and came back with my father's carry-on bag.

"You put it in my bag?" my father asked.

As my mother opened my father's bag, a look of horror
came upon her face. The jam had spilled.

This would have been a mere nuisance for most people but
the fact that it had occurred in my father's bag held monu-
mental significance. My father's complex relationship with
his carry-on bag probably requires psychoanalysis. For as
long as I can remember, his Iran Air bag, which he received
one time when he flew first class, is always packed and ready
to go. It is a constant source of comfort and pride. He keeps
all his personal hygiene products in there, in miniature containers, which he refills constantly. He also keeps his various
eye washes and drops, made necessary by a misdiagnosed and
mistreated childhood bout of trachoma. He keeps clean un-
derclothes, a hand towel, and special cotton swabs for his
eyes, along with a miniature flashlight, extra batteries, and a
radio. Everything is packed in a deliberate manner in neat
rows, the clothes and towel on the bottom, then everything

else by weight. He has shown the contents of this bag to me many, many times, with hope that I, too, will learn his organized ways. He also claims that whenever his bag is searched at the airport, the airline employee comments on the neatness of his bag. I have never believed this story, but it makes my father happy so I just go along with it.

As soon as my mother announced the carrot jam disaster, my father leapt to his feet.

The lid of the jam had come off and everything, from his miniature Listerine container to his Grecian Formula 16 to his clothes, was covered with sticky, orange goo interspersed with slivers of pistachio.

My father turned bright red. "Why did you have to put the stupid jam in *my* bag?" he yelled at my mom, completely forgetting that there were others in the room.

"It was for Fransva," my mother said, invoking the name of her new son-in-law as some sort of human shield.

"Why couldn't you have put it in *your* bag?" my father asked.

"We'll help clean everything," I said.

"Why didn't you put it in a plastic bag?" my father continued.

"I was going to," my mother meekly responded.

"But you didn't," my father continued. "Why didn't you put it in a Ziploc? You put everything else in a Ziploc. You put Ziplocs in Ziplocs. Why didn't you put the jam in a Ziploc?"

It was clear this argument was going to go past New Year's.

François and I tried to help my father clean the bottles, but the Iran Air carry-on bag was ruined. Had we had a crystal ball, we would have told my father that someday he might not want to walk through an American airport with an Iran Air bag, lest he enjoy random checks every time.

My mother was clearly embarrassed that her new son-in-law had just witnessed such an ugly scene. "I'm so sorry, Fransva," she said. "The jam voz for you and so good."

"Maybe he can eat my bag," my father suggested.

"*Baba, basseh*. That's enough," I said, in Persian.

"Speaking of eating," François said, "let's eat!"

"I have to change my clothes first," my father said.

"But you look so nice," François commented.

My father always wears a suit on airplanes. He belongs to the generation for whom airplanes are more than buses in the sky. Flight attendants universally love him, not only for his dapper attire and liberal use of aftershave but because he is probably the only person who compliments them on airplane coffee, every time.

While my father was changing his clothes, François got up. "Maybe I should wear a jacket," he said, adjusting his tie. "You're fine," I assured him.

A few minutes later, my father showed up wearing a velour navy blue jogging suit.

Francois looked at me, perplexed.

The velour navy jogging suit is my male relatives' default attire. I asked my father one time the origins of this de facto uniform and before he could answer, my mother said, "Don't answer. It's gonna be in one of those stories."

As I remember it, back in the early eighties, my uncle Nematollah, always considered the most debonair of the brothers, purchased a velour jogging suit in Las Vegas with the money he had not lost at the blackjack tables. Uncle Nematollah wore his suit everywhere and all the time, with all of us stroking it to see how soft it was while he described its wrinkle-free qualities. Within weeks, my father, his brothers, his brothers-in-law, and some of my cousins had each bought one. This trend spread faster through my family than the flu.

Soon all our gatherings consisted of groups of men in velour touching each other's forearms and discussing prices. "I got it on sale at Robinson's. I went back last week to get a second pair. No mediums left. They go fast."

After all of them had acquired second and, in some cases, third pairs, they started getting catty. "The stripe down the side is girlie," one of my uncles was told. "The brown color looks cheap. Only the navy blue looks good," another was told.

After a few years, most of my younger cousins moved on from the trend, but not my father and several of his brothers. At any given moment, six pairs of velour navy blue jogging suits hang in their closets. Years ago, my father called me one morning to ask me to go to all the local Price Clubs to look for a particularly high-quality velour suit. "They're all out of mediums down here," he explained, sounding desperate.

"I can't do it," I told him.

"Why not?" he asked, rather surprised.

"Because I have a two-year-old and a five-year-old and be-cause you have eight pairs of the same thing already hanging in your closet."

I heard him say something to my mom. Then my mom came on the phone.

"Firoozeh, these are made from really thick velour, highest quality. Your uncle Abdullah just bought one, but he's a small. That's why he found one. Most men don't wear smalls, but he does. The only other size left is the XL. You know how big Americans are. Your dad's not an XL. He's a medium. That's why he's asking you."

"I'm not going," I said.

And it was thus that during Christmas dinner, my father sat across from my husband in one of his many navy blue velour jogging suits.

For the first course, François had made gravlax—salmon cured with vodka, salt, and fresh dill. He served everyone, then started to pour the wine, a dry Alsatian Riesling.

My parents didn't want any wine. I had already told François about this but he hadn't believed me.

"Are you sure you don't want to try a little bit of wine? It really complements the flavor of the food," François said.

"Ve're shoor," my mother said.

My mother picked at her gravlax and asked me in Persian what else there was. "It's not really cooked," she said.

"It's salmon," said François, guessing from my mother's scrunched-up face that there was a problem.

"Eez good," my mother said to him. "I can't eat it," she said to me, in Persian. "What else is there?"

I explained to her, in Persian, that there were several courses. Each would have to be finished before the next one was served. I also told her that a scrunched-up face means the same thing in French and English as it does in Persian.

"Why didn't you tape the lid on the jam jar?" my father asked my mother.

"I did," my mother said.

"I didn't see any tape," my father said. "What kind of tape did you use?"

"Please stop," I told my father.

"I just want to know what kind of tape she used," he persisted. "And this salmon really is raw."

François was, by now, fully aware that my parents did not like the salmon. He cleared the plates, not doing a very good job of hiding his disappointment. My father wanted to keep his fork and knife for the next course. "These are just for the appetizers," François pointed out. "The bigger utensils are for the next course."

"You will end up with so many forks and knives to wash," my father added.

"That's okay," François responded.

The next course—quail stuffed with foie gras and served in a porcini mushroom sauce—evoked oohs and aahs from everyone.

"Vat eez een dees?" my mother asked.

After François explained what foie gras was and how it was made, my parents didn't touch it.

As we ate the quail, everyone was quiet until my father stood up, plate in hand, leaned across the table, and gave his mushrooms to my mom, perhaps as some sort of conciliatory gesture. A huge glob spilled on the white tablecloth. Before I could say, "Don't," my father picked up the glob with his fingers and ate it.

I cleared the plates and had the same conversation about the forks and knives with my father that he had had ten minutes earlier with François, but this time in Persian. My father kept shaking his head.

"Can I talk to you for a moment?" François asked me. We went upstairs. "What's with the jogging suit?" he asked. "And why won't your parents eat anything?"

"The first question requires a long answer," I said. "And the second question, I don't know but I know they think you are a wonderful son-in-law so please overlook their faults. There are many."

Back downstairs, François went in the kitchen to make coffee. "Firoozeh!" he yelled. I ran into the kitchen. "Look!" he said, pointing to the *buche de noel*. I looked at the Yule log, which he had spent hours preparing the day before. The marzipan mushrooms were intact, the dark chocolate crème on top, with its designs to make it look like wood were intact, the chocolate holly leaves were there. I didn't see anything wrong.

"Look inside!" François said.

That's when I noticed that the mocha buttercream filling in the Yule log was missing about two inches on each end. "Your parents ate this while we were upstairs, probably with their fingers," he said.

François cut off the ends of the Yule log that now had no filling and threw them away. He then re-etched the wood design in the chocolate crème on top, trying to hide the damage from the missing ends. The Yule log was now a Yule stump.

The dessert was the one part of the meal my parents ate with gusto. "The inside is the best!" they told François.

"I know you like that part," François told them.

As we cleared the plates, my parents thanked François profusely. "Fransva, tank you so very much. Deh best Chreesmas ever, very best!" my mother said several times.

François and I cleaned the kitchen, while my parents sat on the sofa, looking at the Christmas tree. The Duraflame was still burning.

François took down the Armagnac from the cabinet. "I know your parents won't drink this, but maybe they can just pretend," he said. He arranged the plate of candied orange peels and dark chocolate truffles he had made the day before. As he poured the drinks into tiny glasses, I heard, for the first time, the Ella Fitzgerald record that had been playing in the background the entire evening.

And then I heard my father's voice: "Why didn't you put it in *your* bag?"

Blur

During my first pregnancy, I was employed at a Fortune 500 corporation. It was an entry-level job with generous medical insurance, a subsidized cafeteria, an endless supply of T-shirts, mugs, and Frisbees with the company logo, and a stock option plan that I, having inherited my father's business sense, stayed away from. At the urging of my co-workers, I eventually signed up, but made sure to sell the stock as soon as it went up a few points. With my total gain of twelve hundred dollars, I avoided the whole "sudden millionaire" scenario that later plagued so many of my former colleagues.

During the couple of years I had been employed, I had been through two rounds of layoffs. During one of these layoffs, the only person who lost his job in our department was a blind programmer who was a single father. The sight of him standing in the lobby, his belongings hastily thrown in a box, waiting for a ride, made it clear that I was in the wrong place. For-profit companies are not in the business of charity, but this was a company that spent a six-figure sum annually on indoor plants. I asked the fired man's manager why, of all people, he had to be laid off. She said, "We had to lay off one person, and he was the slowest." Seeing the look of horror on my face, she added, "Yeah, it's a bummer."

From then on, I imagined a sign at the entrance of our company: "Please Check Your Soul at the Door. Pickup Not Necessary."

After the birth of my son, I was offered an exciting new position along with a substantial pay raise. This new position entailed traveling around the world, which is possibly the worst job description for a nursing mom. I turned down the offer and hoped that the world would still be there once I got around to traveling again. I had no doubt I was making the right decision but I was very confused. I belonged, after all, to the generation of Americans who had grown up with the idea of women having it all, but suddenly that philosophy seemed like a well-marketed but unattainable promise of the eighties, like the *Buns of Steel* video.

Motherhood was what every corny cliché promised it would be, with one glaring exception: I have yet to see a coffee mug showing a mother telling her bundle of joy, "I would trade my spleen for another hour of sleep." It is no wonder that sleep deprivation is a kind of torture. By the time my son was two months old, I would have confessed to killing Jimmy Hoffa if it had brought me more sleep.

Perhaps it was appropriate that in my permanent groggy haze, I did not have use of our one car. Public transportation exists where I live, in theory. In practice, it takes two hours and three bus transfers for what takes twenty minutes in a car. This is assuming the buses come on time or at all. It is apparently easier to put a man on the moon than it is to design viable public transportation in California.

Between the sleep deprivation and the lack of transportation, with its ensuing isolation, my life as I knew it came to a screeching halt. Astronauts go through decompression chambers to ensure a smooth transition; new mothers need the postpartum equivalent. Fortunately, my mother came to stay with me for two weeks. She made me *addas polo* (lentil rice), gave me canned peaches, and made sure anything I ate was well cooked and contained no garlic or onions, lest the baby get a tummyache. She also lived with the singular obsession of feeding me watermelon, since it is "good for breast milk." Even though there was a grocery store across the street from our apartment, our building had no elevator, and maneuvering a watermelon up two flights of stairs was beyond her. I was recovering from a Caesarean and even though the doctor had not specifically said, "Don't lug watermelons," I didn't think it would be a good idea. Every day, my mother lamented that "if only we had a watermelon" all would be well. If I complained about lack of sleep, pain from surgery, swollen ankles, my mother had the same response: watermelon.

One day I awoke to find an enormous watermelon on my kitchen counter and my mother smiling like Sylvester after he had finally eaten Tweety.

"Where did this come from?" I asked.

"From the grocery store," she said.

"How did you get it home?"

"Nice man helped me."

My mother explained that the store was having a special: all melons were the same price, regardless of weight. She had noticed an enormous, only-in-America-size watermelon, and bonded with it in a way that only a frugal immigrant can. She then did what any self-respecting mother would do. As she described it, "I looked for a strong man."

According to her, she asked an unsuspecting soul in the fruit aisle if he could "Peh-leaze help for my daw-ter eat vater-melon for baby." This kind, perhaps frightened, gentle giant of a man then carried this super-size fruit across the street, up two flights of narrow stairs, and placed it on my kitchen counter.

"Did you offer to pay him?" I asked.

"I said to him, 'You are verry, verry kind man' and offered him *addas polo.*"

Not surprisingly, the kind man had turned down my mother's offer of lentil rice, lest he then be asked to clean the chimney.

The watermelon was indeed very sweet. I don't know if it actually benefited my breast milk but it made me happy, which benefited everybody. And when my mother left a few days later, she made my husband repeatedly promise to keep me supplied with watermelons, which he did.

Once my mother left, I felt even less capable. This used to be where the extended family came in—sisters, aunts, cousins helping ease the new mother in to her new role—but that sort of support network has gone the way of manual typewriters. I fantasized about Mary Poppins, Mrs. Butterworth, and Enya suddenly appearing and filling my house with the smell of homemade meals, reassuring me with capable, yet gentle voices, insisting I take a nap while they did the housework, singing "Orinoco Flow" until the baby fell asleep or until I understood the lyrics.

In reality, I had no idea what to do with my son. All I knew was that I was completely gaga over him. Other than that, I waited for some primal knowledge to kick in and guide me. I was not about to read any books on child rearing. I had read a few books about pregnancy, which had succeeded in assuring me that I was doing pregnancy all wrong. They didn't make sense to my multicultural brain. I understand the danger of eating raw foods, but what about Japan? Do Japanese women avoid sushi? After a random survey of Japanese people at the local market—that is, those who did not walk away from me or pretend not to speak English—I discovered that, indeed, pregnant Japanese women eat sushi, but only good quality. That made sense. Pregnant French women, I discovered, drink a little bit of wine occasionally, and their children are fine. I immediately got rid of the books, bought sushi, and felt much better.

Taking the same approach to raising my child, I decided that if I just watched my son enough, he would convey all his needs to me. He did. He let me know that he never wanted to sleep. This led to many trips to the pediatrician, who continually assured me that my child was perfectly healthy but was just one of those babies who didn't need a lot of sleep. I didn't even know there was such a category.

So I did what I had to do. I fed him and burped him and cleaned him and took him on walks and tried to get him to nap. Then I fed him and burped him and cleaned him and prayed for him to nap. Then I fed him and burped him and took him on walks and begged him to nap. When he finally did take a nap, I should have rested, since that would be his only nap, but instead I answered the siren song of laundry.

Laundry, oh sweet laundry. I could, at any time during the day or night, be putting clothes in the washing machine, taking clothes out of the washing machine, and putting them in the dryer, folding the ones I had previously taken out of the dryer and deposited in a pile somewhere, or else putting the folded clothes away. I tried my best to make it meaningful. I had read a book about a meditation center where people were given one task, such as chopping bell peppers, for an entire month. This repetition led them to all sorts of enlightening thoughts. Seeking the light, or at least a faint glow, I folded really well. I separated colors. I used the different settings on the washing machine. And at the end of the day, the only thought that entered my head was, "I hate laundry." Being weak, I even resorted to seeking outside approval. I pointed out my stain-removal victories to my husband: "Remember the oatmeal stain on the onesie? Gone!"

If only doing laundry brought any sort of satisfaction, the lives of mothers across the world would be so much better. But alas, laundry baskets, unlike bank accounts, fill up quickly and empty slowly. Every time I caught a glimpse of my empty laundry basket, I knew what the mailman felt at the end of each day when he looked at his vacant mail bag. The joy is overshadowed by the knowledge that soon there will be something in it, and within a day, possibly hours if bedsheets have to be changed because baby's digestive tract did not like green beans, it will be completely full again.

Maybe in the days of yore, when women went down to the river to wash clothes, they at least benefited from female bonding and communal kvetching. I am not suggesting trading in modern conveniences, but laundry would be more enjoyable in the company of another, and no, those people handing out copies of *Watchtower* at the Laundromat do not qualify.

My first year as a mother was tough, like one of those births where the baby is facing the wrong way and the doctor decides to manually turn him. In my case, it took about a year for me to get straightened out. Yes, I tried to start conversations in the produce aisle. ("I see you're buying iceberg lettuce. Remember the seventies, when iceberg was king? Now there's butter, bibb, frisee, romaine . . .")

It didn't work.

I remember vowing to do upper-arm exercises ten minutes a day.

I didn't.

I remember wanting to make homemade baby food.

I didn't.

I remember desperately wanting to be better than who I was.

But every once in a while, I look at my son's photo album from his first year and all I see is a baby who knew he was loved. I see a baby who was fed, cleaned, and clothed. I see a baby who went on walks around his neighborhood and saw lots of squirrels. I see a baby who loved Persian nursery rhymes (*"attal, mattal, tootooleh . . ."*). And I see a baby who did not care that his mom's buns were not made of steel.

You Had a Bad Day

When our children were one and four, my husband and I purchased a two-bedroom, one-bath fixer-upper. Since we could barely afford the mortgage, moving out of the house during renovations was not an option. Ever resourceful, we decided to build a room and bathroom behind our garage and move in there. Once we were finished with the house, that room would become my parents' room.

When the renovation started, we moved into our new abode as planned and put most of our belongings in the garage. The room that we were to live in for the next four months held a bunk bed for the kids, a large mattress on the floor, toys, essential dishes, a microwave oven, and piles of clothes. If Zen had an antonym, it would be that room.

Our renovation coincided with my husband's new job. At the time, Silicon Valley was in the throes of the second gold rush, known as the High-Tech Boom. The mailman, the dental hygienist, everyone but us, was taking a stroll on Easy Street, making money buying stocks in what seemed like random companies making random things. There were even stories of people buying stocks in the wrong companies and still making money. ("I meant to buy Cisco stock but I made a typo. By the time I realized my mistake, I'd made twenty grand!")

Aside from the unprecedented number of people making vast amounts of money, what was even more amazing about this second gold rush was the demographics of the players. Indians, Iranians, Chinese, black, white, vegetarian, atheist, Jewish, Christian, Muslim—high-tech companies resembled ads for Benetton, although not as good-looking. And like Benetton, the clothing of these pioneers, given to them for free by their companies, all had logos and slogans meant to tantalize and excite all those in the Kingdom of Technology.

"G4 TECHTU!"

"We Achieve 22 Teraflops!"

"Do You Yahoo?"

My husband's new job was in a start-up company that specialized in "middleware." On two dozen occasions, using charts and graphs, my husband explained to me what that means. I have no retention on that topic. I hear "middleware," I see corsets, girdles, and brassieres.

Like all employees of start-ups, a portion of his compensation consisted of stock options, meaning that if the company went public, those stock options could be sold, hopefully for oodles of money. This was the dream that fueled Silicon Valley.

The CEO of my husband's company was a single Indian man. He had been involved in a couple of fairly successful start-ups, but that wasn't what he wanted. Bill Gates was the new Gandhi, and this boss's dreams consisted not of inner balance but of the enormous kind in the bank.

His apartment was across the street from the office, allowing him the luxury of going home only to shower, and not every day. The office was stocked with food and caffeine in various forms, all of which served the same purpose as a ball and chain. The boss even had a small cot in his office, where he spent most nights.

He was certainly not alone in his maniacal zeal for success. Working nonstop and abandoning one's life were marks of success in the Valley, giving employees bragging rights. No employee worth his stock options would ever claim to want to go home to see the kids before bedtime, or at least not do so openly. Not surprisingly, it wasn't just the high-tech lawyers in the Valley who did well. Divorce lawyers could not bill fast enough.

But even among crazy dedicated people, my husband's boss seemed a bit off. He was known for e-mails telling his employees that if they wanted to talk to him, "anytime after 10:00 PM would work." He also once sent a company memo letting everyone know that all employees were getting December 25 off. Never mind that it's a national holiday. He continued: December 24 was not a holiday, but, he was giving everyone that afternoon off. The best part, however, was that on Christmas Eve, as we sat down to eat the meal that I, a Muslim woman who technically should have had the day off, had prepared by myself, the phone rang. It was crazy boss with a technical question that could not wait.

But we put up with all this because as soon as the company went public and everyone bought middleware, whatever the heck that was, we would be on Easy Street and not in a cramped space.

Living in one room had many drawbacks. The worst was that as soon as one person awoke, so did everybody else. Our children, descended not from apes but roosters, made sure that we never missed an early morning.

One Sunday, my son woke up first as always. Within a few minutes, my husband was in the shower, getting ready for the usual Sunday at the office. I got dressed, trying to muster some enthusiasm for the long day that lay ahead of me. I had recently read about a new bagel shop that had opened near our house. I decided this was the day to support a new business.

I put the kids in the double stroller and off we went. It was 6:30 AM.

Not surprisingly, we were the only patrons in the store. We purchased our bagels and sat by ourselves in the dining area, which was separated from the rest of the shop by a wall. It was a lovely scene worthy of Norman Rockwell. The bagels kept the children busy while I read the paper, every once in a while saying "uh, huh" or "yeah," to give the kids the impression that I was listening to them. After twenty minutes, they were done. In America, bagels, cars, and behinds are bigger than in other places, so I went to find a container for the remainders. I left my keys on the table with my children.

By then, there were several other patrons in line, so I waited while the lone sixteen-year-old employee filled the orders. Suddenly, I saw my son walking toward me with what looked like blood all over his shirt, face, and sleeves. I knew it wasn't blood because I had been gone for maybe only five minutes. As soon as my son saw me, though, he started to cry, holding up his hand. It was blood.

Turns out he had been playing with my key chain, which held a small Swiss Army knife in case of emergencies—or in this case, to cause emergencies. He had opened the knife and upon attempting to close it, had stabbed himself near his thumb, which, like the lip area, bleeds *a lot*. He had tried to wipe the blood by using his shirt, hence the blood all over his shirt and sleeves. He had also tried to wipe his tears, hence the blood on his face. All this in less than five minutes, and his hand was still bleeding.

The two things I retained from nine years as a Girl Scout were "Do not panic" and that Thin Mints taste best frozen. I went to the counter with my son and asked for their first aid kit. One look at my bloody son and it became clear that this employee had never been a scout. "Oh my God!" she screamed and froze.

I reached over the counter, grabbed a pile of napkins, and applied pressure to the cut. It actually worked. The bleeding slowed down. My son's crying sped up.

I held him close, stroking his hair, which had also gotten bloody, and assured him that it would be all right. Even though our Norman Rockwell morning had turned into a Hieronymus Bosch triptych, everything would be fine now. I took him back to the dining area.

My daughter was gone.

There were two doors in the dining area. One for the bathroom, which she could not have opened by herself, and the other a swinging door leading to the kitchen area, which said, "Employees Only." I pushed open the swinging door, and there she was, surrounded by the freshly baked bagels she had purloined from the trays she could reach.

I grabbed her and went back to the table with my son, whose bleeding had now stopped but who was looking very pale. I knew I needed to calm him, so I started telling him a story about the monkey that escaped and hid on our balcony in Tehran when I was a little girl. After a few minutes, my son looked at his shirt, then looked at me and said, "There's so much blood everywhere. I feel . . . sick." Then he turned green. I grabbed him and ran out of the store. I flung open the door. Exactly where a welcome mat might have been, he threw up.

When I walked back in the store, the first thing I saw was the employee walking toward me with a mop, a look of horror on her face again.

"I am so sorry," I said. "We'll be leaving now."

I grabbed my daughter, put them both in the stroller, and started to walk home. It was 7:30 AM.

When we arrived home to our one room, I changed my son's outfit, washed the blood and vomit from his face and arms, changed my own clothes, then put everything in the sink to remove the mélange of stains. My son was still quite shaken, so I put him on the mattress and started to tell him the story about the first time I dropped him off at preschool and how well he handled it and how poorly I handled it. I had told him this story many times and it always made him laugh. It worked this time, too.

Hearing him laugh soothed my own nerves, but then I suddenly remembered my daughter. During the duration of my story, I had been facing my son and the wall and hadn't heard a peep out of my daughter.

I turned around. In the middle of the room, on our brand new carpet, stood my one-year-old, diaper off, looking very pleased at her output. She had never done this before. She had chosen this day, this moment, to learn to remove her diaper.

I didn't think of cleaning up the mess. I picked up the

phone and called my husband. When I heard his voice, I started to cry, which I usually do only at movies and weddings, watching certain commercials, at graduations, during John Denver songs, and at funerals.

"What's wrong? Are the kids all right? Did something happen?" he asked, completely panic-stricken.

"I'm not sure where to begin. The kids are all right but it's a *really* bad day."

"I'll be home," he said.

My daughter's gift required professional carpet cleaning.

Shortly thereafter, our renovations were finally finished. We moved back into the main house with its two bedrooms, which now seemed downright chateaulike.

And as for my parents' room, my parents never slept in it. The first time they saw it, my mother said, "It's not a part of the house." She was right. The two were separated by fifty feet.

After we moved into our remodeled home, my husband's company laid off half of its employees, including him. We didn't make any money on the stock options, but we did have to pay taxes on them, thanks to something called the Alternative Minimum Tax.

The good news was that whenever our mailman or dental hygienist complained about the taxes they had to pay on their gains, we told them our story and they immediately felt better. We were their Prozac. And maybe that's the antidote for all bad days: find someone with a worse day. They're out there.

Past the Remote

Sometime after the birth of our second child, I decided to get rid of our TV. I kept this thought to myself, knowing it would not be embraced by anyone else in my household. Finally, one day, during a commercial break, I shared my idea with the Frenchman, who didn't like it. "Think about it," I told him, "we can actually have conversations that last longer than three commercials, raise kids who will be responsible for their own entertainment, and do whatever else humans did before twenty-four-hour TV."

He didn't say anything but I knew what he was thinking. "*X-Files* is just a show," I added. "Your life will be just as rich without it. And if it's not, then we have bigger problems than we realize."

My husband and I had both been raised without TV as a

major influence, until we came to America. In Abadan, our home had access to one Iranian station and one from Kuwait, not as many choices as those sophisticated city folks living in Tehran, who actually had two Iranian stations and one American station. In Abadan, we could choose from about seven hours of daily programming, starting from around 4:00 PM until 11:00 PM. We could watch the news, Persian movies from popular artists such as Parviz Sayyad, or American shows such as *Ironside, Bonanza, Bewitched, Flipper, Star Trek, Lost in Space,* or *I Dream of Jeannie,* all dubbed in Persian. One of the most popular shows was *The Fugitive,* which my brothers watched every week, hoping each week that the one-armed man would be caught.

If someone turned on the TV before four o'clock in the afternoon, there was static. After eleven, more static. People were forced to have a life, or at least get some sleep.

I used to watch thirty minutes of American cartoons per week, and I enjoyed it more than any kid I know today who has access to nonstop cartoons. Whoever said less is more had lived in Abadan.

François had been raised in Paris in a family devoted to the daily news. Because of homework and a strict bedtime, he was usually able to watch only the first thirty minutes of most movies on TV. During the first few years of our marriage, he rented a lot of movies and was particularly thrilled to watch beyond the first half hour, all the way to the end.

After much cajoling, my husband agreed to a two-step detox program. Step one involved putting the TV in the garage for one month. François wanted to shorten this step to one week, but I held firm. "Don't fool yourself," I told him. "It will take at least a month for Mulder and Xena to leave your bloodstream."

Step two entailed getting rid of the TV permanently, but only if step one was a total success.

We hauled the TV, VCR, the various remote controls, and the TV cabinet to the garage. Suddenly, our living room looked much bigger, but the air seemed heavier, like the last day of a long vacation.

Our children, like most kids of a certain age, were accustomed to watching public television in the morning. I had never watched *Sesame Street* or *Mr. Rogers' Neighborhood* as a child, since they were not broadcast in Iran. It was not until I became a mother that I found myself enchanted by Elmo, Oscar the Grouch, Big Bird, and Fred Rogers and his gentle ways. These shows are a valid reason for *having* a TV. However, even with quality programming, it's easy to overdo screen time. If the television screen went blank after *Sesame Street* and *Mister Rogers'*, that would be ideal, but it didn't. There was always another program coming up, and it was always a program that my kids wanted to watch. Needing more time for housework, I wasn't exactly anxious to turn off the electric babysitter. It's not as if my children were watching a Jean-Claude Van Damme marathon, but I still felt guilty. Just as too many carrots turn skin yellow, too many TV programs, even the good ones, can turn kids into creatures whose favorite phrase is "Can we see what's next?"

Once the television disappeared from the house, I prepared myself for the Whine Festival. Surprisingly, the absence of our TV was not met with much dismay from my kids. They immediately found something else to do in the mornings, as if they already had a Plan B but had never had to use it. However, their morning activities now involved me in a way that was more time-consuming than my turning on the TV and leaving the room. If I put the kitchen chairs in the living room, put a blanket over them and called it a tent, I had time to empty the dishwasher and start dinner. If I equipped this tent with empty plastic food containers, wooden spoons, and stacks of towels, I could finish making dinner. If I gave them bananas to peel and mash for banana bread, I had another ten minutes, and a mess. Having a TV was definitely easier, and less messy, but I had a nagging feeling that I would eventually pay for that ease later. I wanted my children to be masters of their own fun, to know that their imaginations were richer than any TV show or computer or video game. I knew that imagination, like any muscle, needs to be exercised, or else one ends up with the mental equivalent of a beer belly. With television, my children often had access to the product of talented writers, actors, and puppeteers, but they were just passive participants. I don't know if one benefits in any way from just watching a lot of TV. I have never heard of anyone making a deathbed confession: "My biggest regret? Missing season four of *Law and Order.*"

I was trying to re-create the same kind of boring childhood I had had, the kind of childhood that had forced me to notice insects, draw flowers, and collect Corn Flakes boxes so I could stack them to build houses. I constantly made up games because there was absolutely nothing else to do. I played with buttons, tea sets, and empty Nivea containers; I hung out in the kitchen and watched food being prepared. I absorbed the adult world around me, then replayed it all with my dolls, with myself cast as the grown-up with all the answers. Boredom was my empty canvas.

Without our television, the Frenchman suffered more than our children. A tent in the living room did not excite him; and neither did the ice-melting contests, complete with clipboards and stopwatches, that worked wonders for the kids. In the evenings, I tried to be fascinating, but it's hard to compete with Agent Mulder, Xena, and a coterie of women wearing breastplates. I did, however, make the effort to make nicer-than-usual meals and have his favorite bottles of wine. Despite my best efforts, he looked forlorn, like someone with jet lag. I figured with enough food and wine, he'd be fine, eventually.

For me, the toughest part of living sans television was folding laundry. I always dumped the pile of clean clothes in front of the television set, and folded while watching something—anything really. Without television, I discovered that folding clothes is really, *really* boring.

Once I realized that I needed something, anything, while I folded, I remembered that old standby from the days of yore: the radio. I tuned in to National Public Radio and the BBC and immediately gained a few IQ points. Listening to the news on reputable stations did have its drawbacks. There was virtually no coverage of Zsa Zsa Gabor. Having lived in Southern California, I was used to breaking news being defined as Zsa Zsa Gabor and her hairdresser hitting a utility pole while driving in Los Angeles. This bit of news, along with a pastiche of her career, had preempted the news about a bombing in Kenya. But then again, Africa came into existence for the American media only once Angelina Jolie went there.

Listening to the BBC had other advantages. Americans have a simplistic love affair with British accents, claiming that they make everything sound better. I am here to confirm that this is, in fact, entirely true. No matter how bleak the news may be, when reported with the crisp, erudite British accent of a good-looking, intelligent journalist wearing a Burberry trench coat, it gives one hope. Of course, with radio, one cannot be sure that the reporters are indeed attractive, but they sure do sound like it. And that's all a woman needs to fold some laundry.

We hit only one major snag during our TV-free month. My son came home one day quite distraught, having been told by his classmates that he was not allowed to play Power Rangers. The Power Rangers game, as played in his preschool, involved a group of boys who staked their claim each morning by announcing, "I am the blue Power Ranger! I am the red Power Ranger," then kicking the air and grunting. My son, having never seen the show but wanting desperately to play, had announced, "I am the brown Power Ranger!" which had immediately stopped everyone mid-kick. There is no brown Power Ranger. In the scheme of life, this is a minor faux pas, but I couldn't convince my son. I even told him that brown was a very logical guess—it's not like he had guessed "turquoise with a pattern"—but he was inconsolable.

A quick trip to Target, and he was the proud owner of Power Rangers underwear, depicting the various correct colors worn by the characters, with brown not being one of them. To restore his confidence, I let him in on a secret: "The power is in the underwear." This led to many days of happy playing at school, until I received a phone call from his teacher, which led to another valuable life lesson: "Don't show your underwear to everyone."

Once our television-free month ended, François admitted that he liked it. "I have so much more time," he said, rather surprised. I loved not having a TV for many reasons, including feeling countercultural, despite living in the suburbs, wearing comfortable shoes, and driving a station wagon. Amazingly, our children had finally noticed our backyard, which had never beckoned them before. They surprised me with their new-found creativity. My daughter had discovered that junk mail could be cut and glued and made into all sorts of artwork, defined in our household as anything made by our children. We became perhaps the only family in America who looked forward to unsolicited credit card applications. My parents, however, suffered. They were on the receiving end of countless "gifts" made of coupon books and Pottery Barn catalogs.

My mother solved this by displaying the grandchildren's artwork in the garage, so she could see the artwork whenever she went in there. My children felt this was extra special since nobody else's grandparents taped artwork on the washing machine and dryer, especially the side facing the wall.

With my husband's blessing, I put an ad in the paper to sell our television set. The first person who came was a Japanese physician, who in very broken English told me that he was conducting research at our local university hospital for two years. He hoped to improve his English by watching television. I told him I would be happy to offer the TV, VCR, and cabinet for twenty dollars, even though I had advertised the set for eighty. "You will be healing people in two languages," I told him. This led to much confusion, until he took out a large wad of twenty-dollar bills and told me to take what I wanted. I took a twenty, and he was very, very happy, expressing the universal glee of a successful bargain hunt. He also gave me a piece of paper and asked me to suggest some good shows. I wrote "*Marcus Welby, M.D.*—Find on cable." He smiled and put the piece of paper in his pocket, along with his wad of cash. I like to think that somewhere in Tokyo there is a bilingual physician with a fabulous bedside manner.

Twelve years later, the only people who have yet to adjust to our TV-free home are my parents. My father still likes to ask us if we have gotten rid of any other modern conveniences. "You still have indoor plumbing?" he regularly asks. This joke was funny ten years ago, but my father repeats it every time he visits.

The only time we regret not having a TV is on Oscar night. We have solved this by inviting ourselves to other people's houses, under the guise of "Let's have an Oscar party!" followed by "At your house!" It works every time.

The single biggest advantage during the past years has been what my children have not seen, namely thousands and thousands of commercials. Unlike with me, who spent half of my time in America whining for the next Barbie or Weeble accessory, my children's wants are their own, and have nothing to do with marketing firms planting ideas in their heads. I never needed a Pet Rock, and I would like to take this opportunity to apologize to my father for making him buy me one, along with the accessory that turned it into a necklace, and then promising not to tell my mother, which I did.

Whenever my children are asked to make a list of gifts for their birthdays or other occasions, they come up with a maximum of three items. One year, I told my son that if he learned to go across the monkey bars, I would buy him any toy he wanted. He came home from school the next day brimming with excitement. One of his classmates had suggested an enormous toy store but my son couldn't remember the name. He thought real hard. "It's called We Are Toys," he finally said. "You mean, Toys'R'Us," I corrected him. "You've heard of it?" he said, completely surprised.

"I think so," I told him.

He thought I was really cool. This is a good thing, since not having a TV is not generally considered cool, at least not according to some people who think watching *The Price Is Right* is the highlight of each day.

And to that aforementioned individual, yes, we still have indoor plumbing.

In the Closet

My cousin Mehrdad and his family recently drove up for a visit. They live near my parents and are among the few remaining people who consider car trips with children "vacations," extolling the opportunity to bond and make lasting memories. My family is grateful for Mehrdad's embrace of simpler times. Coupled with his generous character and ownership of a van, he is our favorite de facto long-distance mover. For a few mortadella sandwiches and a six-pack of Sprite, my mother regularly stuffs any remaining air pockets of Mehrdad's van with treasures from her closets, ostensibly for "Firoozeh and Fransva."

Before Mehrdad's arrival last week, my mother called me three times a day for two weeks to go over the inventory of goods she planned to send, in her signature stream-of-consciousness style. "I'm sending the vase I bought for Nas-

rin's shower. I ended up giving her a spice rack. Your aunt
Jaleh also gave her a vase. Thank goodness I gave her a spice
rack. Do you need any saffron?" In my younger days, I used
to listen to the items, their provenance, and all the unrelated
tangents and then tell her that I wasn't interested. This resulted in her sending me all the goods "in case I changed my
mind." As I've gotten older and accepted that I will never win
any argument with my mother, I listen and meekly agree with
everything she says. Our relationship has never been so good.

Mehrdad arrived at our house carrying a huge duffel bag
and two powder-blue Samsonite suitcases, circa 1968. I
waited until he and his family left before I started excavat-
ing the bags. I wasn't sure that Mehrdad would have appreciated the exact nature of some of the treasures he had hauled,
such as the ten-pound bag of basmati rice. My mother had
explained to me earlier that the rice was the result of a "Buy
five ten-pound bags of basmati rice and receive a free rice
cooker!" special at the Iranian supermarket. Never mind that
my father had strained his back carrying fifty pounds of rice
to the car and then from the car to the house. "With all the recent wedding showers, an extra rice cooker in the closet just
made sense," my mother explained, "but I don't need the
rice, so I gave two bags to Mahtab, one to Aunt Sedigeh, and
one to you. I kept one for us, for guests, of course. We don't
eat white rice anymore." This declaration was punctuated by
my father's voice in the background: "I hate brown rice."

"It's good for you," my mother reminded him.

"I'd rather just not eat," my father continued.

I reminded them that this was a long-distance call and they
could argue for free later.

My mother then explained that she would be sending me a
"few things that Fransva might like." This is my mother's

way of saying that she is sending stuff I don't want, but using the Frenchman as an excuse.

Before my mother's knees started bothering her, she and my dad went on a few trips, courtesy of my brother Farshid. Everywhere they went, they managed to buy the kind of souvenirs that beg the question "Who would buy this?"—from Singapore, a bouquet of plastic orchids; from Japan, a clown with the word "Tokyo" on its distended belly; from London, an umbrella with the phrase "Fresh as a Daisy" written all around the edge. This umbrella, with its catchy phrase conjuring images of feminine hygiene products, was made of clear plastic, except for the giant yellow daisies emblazoned across the top.

Each of these items was displayed with such enthusiasm that I had to suppress the nagging urge to throw them away. I secretly hoped that if we kept them long enough, they would someday inexplicably come into fashion, like headbands, or else become the kind of stuff that becomes desirable over time, like Bob's Big Boy paraphernalia. Sadly, the market for plastic clowns from Tokyo is still dormant.

During this most recent closet cleaning, my mother sent us the cheese plate she had bought from Holland. "Cheese plate from Holland" sounds innocuous, but so does brown recluse spider. The cheese plate was a slab of wood with a faux tile glued on. The tile depicted a Dutch couple, their arms around each other in a stiff embrace that led one to think that either the artist did not know how to draw bent arms or else the Dutch are not touchy-feely. Behind the couple are two windmills, a creek, and two rowboats. Both the man and the woman are wearing matching clogs. I could have made peace with all this were it not for the word "Holland" written in large letters on the bottom. It's not like someone could have mistaken the scene for "Cairo," but nonetheless, the manufacturer probably thought that the kind of person who buys this sort of souvenir might forget which country the windmills, clogs, and stiff embrace represented.

My mother also returned several gifts I had given her over the years. This may sound callous, but gift-giving in my family is a flexible concept with many loopholes. This is partly because in the Iranian culture, people are always exchanging gifts. Aside from the usual birthdays and graduations, we also believe that pretty much anytime we go to someone's house, we must enter with a gift. Those of us who immigrated to the United States have also adopted the American idea of baby and wedding showers, which include gifts, and wedding anniversaries, which mean more gifts. The idea of celebrating marriage anniversaries was completely foreign to my family, since most marriages were arranged and did not come with the requisite romantic story of how we met and where we went on our first date and the first time we kissed. It just initially seemed odd to celebrate the day that "our families decided we should marry even though I had never met you and, frankly, it's not working out so well." But showing that immigrant ability to adapt, we've embraced that one, too, even if there are no Hallmark cards that speak to arranged marriages: "Roses are red, violets are blue, on the day we got married, I couldn't stand you."

All this gift giving is fine and dandy if your last name is Rockefeller, but for most people on a fixed budget, this aspect of our culture leads to another: the fine art of regifting. This means that whenever certain relatives receive an unwanted gift, they just save it for someone else. Some people are more nuanced at this than others. I learned early on that most gifts that came in Neiman Marcus boxes were not from Neiman Marcus; they were usually from that other Neiman Marcus, Marshalls. One must also be careful to remove the original gift card, a faux pas that, like catching your husband in bed with another woman, defies any explanation.

In the case of my mother, she was passing the gifts to me, the original giver. She did, however, let me know that I was free to pass them along. I now have to decide which of my friends is worthy of the "As seen on TV" garnishing set that I gave my mother sometime before the fall of the Berlin Wall. This gift, which comes in a box adorned with a picture of a watermelon turned into a Viking ship, represents the kind of spontaneous project any mother could embrace between picking up the kids at school, making dinner, and getting sixty minutes of aerobic exercise. Frankly, I don't think any of my friends is worthy.

I also received some souvenirs from my wedding. My wedding dress, however, was not among them. "There was no more room in Mehrdad's van," my mother said, "unless he removed the seats." My mother did, however, send my wedding headdress, a three-part beaded contraption that, at the time, had seemed chic and fashion-forward. This was, however, the eighties, a decade that introduced us to pouffy sleeves and gold lamé, both of which were in abundant display at my wedding. The beaded headdress is now referred to in my house as part of the "Oksana Baiul Wedding Collection."

Along with the headdress, I also received thirty beaded flower party favors, which were supposed to have been handed out during the Persian portion of my wedding, in 1989. My mother admitted that, at the time, she could not part with them. The candied almonds have partially disintegrated, and the beaded flowers are yellowed and droopy. They are now in my closet.

My mother also sent the last remaining photo albums with pictures from Iran. Over the years, she and my father used to look at these photos and talk about going back and visiting friends and family. This year they took what they said is their last trip to Iran. It is simply too exhausting for them, both physically and emotionally. It pains them to see Iran in its present condition, with its skyrocketing inflation and a younger generation with no future. My parents have not taken a single picture during any of their trips back. They prefer looking at photos of the past. It is the Iran they want to remember, the Iran that held so much promise.

When my mother gave me the last of the photo albums, she said she was giving them to me so I could write about them. I told her I would. I also told her that I would write about the ten-pound bag of rice. "What is there to write about a ten-pound bag of rice?" she wanted to know. "Plenty," I assured her.

I do not know what else remains in my mother's closets. Every time I receive a shipment, I am convinced it is the last one. "Is there anything left?" I ask her. "I'm almost done," she says every time. I am now convinced that she holds on to things for the same reason we hold on tight during roller-coaster rides; we think we have to. Perhaps with every shipment to my house, she's letting go a little bit. And perhaps she sees that even when she lets go and unexpected things happen, like a revolution that displaces her forever, she still does not fall off.

My closets, however, are getting very full.

Seeing Red

In high school, one of my closest friends was Susan. Aside from being very, very funny, Susan deserves credit for teaching me everything I know about the Jewish culture. Even though I already knew the nuts and bolts of Judaism, it was at Susan's house where I first tasted a latke, and realized that any religion where fried potatoes is part of the tradition is good. I also learned when and how to say "oy," and grasped the concept of "chutzpah," a guiding force to this day.

When we lived in Iran, we had many Jewish friends. There were, and still are, more Jews living in Iran than in any other country in the Middle East outside of Israel. It was no surprise that everything Susan ever told me about the Jewish culture felt familiar.

One day Susan mentioned something about "a Jewish mother." Even though I had heard the term before, I asked for the exact meaning. "It's all about guilt," she said. As she started to elaborate, complete with examples of Jewish mothers she had known, I was shocked. "That's not a Jewish mother," I told her. "That's my mother."

Growing up, I assumed all parents used guilt as one of the key pillars of parenting. My mother was so stealthy that you never knew what hit you. It was like Andre Agassi's serve. You can know it's coming toward you, but there's still nothing you can do. Andre Agassi is, coincidentally, half Iranian. It is entirely possible that his serve is nothing more than guilt redirected.

I had always been familiar with guilt and its powers, but never more acutely than during my high school years. These years coincided with the aftermath of the Iranian Revolution. My father had lost his job, and companies were not scrambling to hire Iranian men with unpronounceable names and thick accents. The few jobs he did find were in other cities, so my father moved around while my mother and I stayed in Southern California. My brother Farshid chose to attend a college nearby so he could live at home with us. Without his sacrifice, my mother and I would have had to return to Iran. Living on our own was out of the question.

This was not a happy time in my life, coinciding with high school and adolescence, which are also not happy times. The constant beacons of light in my life were my friends. Like any other adolescent, I loved to hang out with them. The problem was that hanging out with my friends meant that I was not hanging out with my mom. My brother wasn't home very much since he was attending college and working. His absence was understandable and expected. Mine wasn't. Here was my mother, making the sacrifice to stay in America because of me, and I was abandoning her at every possible moment. (Say "oy" now.) I knew all this, and felt the guilt, but I was fifteen and really wanted to spend the night at Mary Ann's so we could discuss all the boys we liked, and try to figure out why they never, ever liked us back. We never solved that one.

The guilt scenario was always the same. One of my friends would call and invite me to spend the night. I would ask my mother for permission. The response was always the same: silence followed by a faint "Do whatever you want." That was the first ace.

As soon as I started to pack, my mother would appear at my door. "When are you coming back?" she'd ask. I always said, "I'm not sure." I said this to limit the worrying, not that that was even possible. I had learned the hard way that if I said, "I'll be back at nine" but got home at 9:15, my mother would let me know that for fifteen minutes she had nothing but visions of car accidents, lightning, shark attacks—you name it.

Given that I didn't smoke or drink, always got good grades, and hung out with an oddly responsible crowd whose worst crime was baking too much, I found my mother's excessive worrying to be beyond annoying, but I still felt terribly guilty. I knew that in her eyes and the eyes of her generation of Iranians, I was a horrible daughter. A dutiful daughter would stay home and keep her mother company. But I just couldn't help wanting to go to Mary Ann's or Carolyn's or Carol's or Karen's or Ruthie's or Susan's, where things were always rosier than at my house. Without my friends, I would have more than likely ended up as one of those adults living with and relating mostly to animals, and not in a glamorous way like Brigitte Bardot.

Despite my mother's guilt, I still managed to live a life, at least on the outside, that did not look too different from that of my American friends. The guilt was like a ball and chain that wasn't quite heavy enough to keep me back, but loud enough that I could always hear it clanging.

I realized years later that my mother's use of guilt was her way of trying to corral me within the confines of her world. Like many immigrants, she was afraid that the unknown road I was taking would leave me with nothing but regrets. Even though her own life had not always turned out as she would have wanted, she wanted me to follow the same familiar road. At least then my regrets would be similar to hers.

Ironically, today my life, on the outside, is not that different from hers. I'm a stay-at-home mom of three, I cook dinner every night, and am rather domestically inclined by American standards. But I took my own road to get here, a road that empowered me with a college education and allowed me to marry the man of my choosing. I traveled, pursued interests, and got lost sometimes, but having made my own decisions means that I cannot blame my parents when something goes wrong in my life, an option that I sorely miss.

When I got married, my relationship with my mother improved enormously. For her, the fact that a nice man with a college education and no prison record wanted to marry me lifted an enormous burden from her life. After my engagement, my mother even made a point of telling my future husband what she considered my most annoying trait, just to make sure he knew what he was getting: "She reads all deh time. Non-estop."

"I do, too," he said.

A few months after our wedding, a day that my mother declared "the best day of their lives and the best wedding ever," my parents decided to come for a visit. By now they had watched the three-and-a-half-hour wedding video enough times to give us cause for concern. "I keep it in my purse. Wherever we go, everyone wants to see it," my mother had told us. "Too bad you don't have a TV," she repeated, hoping we would borrow one from a neighbor. Unfortunately, during their stay with us, we told my parents, they would not be able to watch us on tape but would have to settle for watching us live.

My mother also kept telling us that she was coming with a surprise. "What is it?" I kept asking her. She refused to divulge.

When we picked them up at the airport, all of us hugging and kissing while my mother cried, my father told my husband that he was happy that we were still married. "At this point, no returns on the wife, just exchanges. I have two sons," he said, introducing my husband to his unique brand of humor.

While we waited at the luggage carousel, my mother reminded us of the "soorprize." Suddenly, we saw an enormous package struggling to come out of the tube that emptied onto the luggage carousel. It couldn't come out. It was jammed. It was like a ten-pound baby being born to a petite woman. Yellow lights started to flash. An airline employee ran up the ramp to yank the package out. I knew that whatever impractical object that was, it was linked to my mother. "What is it?" I asked. "Soorprize for Fransva," was the only cryptic message she would share.

By the time we picked "it" up, we knew it was bedding. Due to the layers of large plastic bags and tape, we had to wait to arrive home to see it. On the way home, my mother elaborated: "Fransva, you have good taste. I buy dis Ralph Lauren for you. I know you like. Most beautifool. I know you like."

François, ever naïve, responded with "Yes, I love Ralph Lauren. That is very generous of you!"

This may have seemed like a legitimate response, but it was the equivalent of double-bolting the fire escape. The Frenchman, untrained in the ways of guilt, had eliminated any possible out. We were doomed.

After arriving home, we unwrapped the bedding. It was red, bright, bright red, and very fluffy in a bad way. My mother was watching us like a hawk. "So beautifool," she said. "I loook all over for you," she told us, cementing the guilt.

I hated it, as would have anybody else not working at Mustang Ranch.

My husband and I went in our bedroom, taking *It* with us to put on the bed to make my mother happy. My husband whispered, "No way is this Ralph Lauren. It's ugly."

It wasn't just ugly. It was loud and ugly. I remembered reading that one of the astronauts claimed that the Great Wall of China was the only man-made object visible from outer space. Now there was something else.

François looked at the tag to see if it was misspelled. "Ralph Lauren does not make anything this horrible," he said.

"Maybe Ralph was guilted into hiring his no-talent cousin for the summer and this is the result," I suggested.

Regardless, we were stuck with *It*. Thanks to my husband's ill-timed compliment for Ralph Lauren products, there was nothing we could do but fake enthusiasm, which was not easy.

My mother spent the next few days repeating her mantra of how beautifool it was and how she knew Fransva appreciated Ralph Lauren and how much she had looked to find something so beautifool.

After they left, my husband said, "We have to get rid of *It*."

"We can't just get rid of *It*," I told him. "We'll never hear the end of it." It was clear that when it came to guilt, his Catholic background had ill prepared him, regardless of claims otherwise.

"Something has to happen to it," I told him.

"A theft?" he suggested.

"Who would ever steal *this*?" I said, trying to sound educational and not angry.

We came up with many possible scenarios, from the neighbor's dog mauling it to blueberries staining it to losing it while on a picnic in Golden Gate Park. But none would have passed muster with my mother.

Finally, we came up with a clever idea. We decided to wash it so many times that it would fade and then we could donate it guilt-free to a homeless person.

Every week, as I hauled our clothes to the Laundromat, I took the comforter and an extra roll of quarters. I washed it in hot water and dried it thoroughly on the highest setting. As I watched it go round and round in the dryer, I thought about Ralph Lauren and my attempts to destroy what was undoubtedly a counterfeit. I knew that my mother had bought the comforter in good faith, but fakes are bad for the economy, I told myself. Even though what I was doing was bad for my mother, it was good for mankind. If Mr. Lauren could see me now, he would probably reward me with a real Ralph Lauren comforter. Maybe he would also give me an entire Ralph Lauren wardrobe or invite me on a duck hunt. Afterward, still in our jodhpurs, we would sit on rattan furniture, surrounded by beautiful people looking forlornly in opposite directions. Maybe we would become friends and he would give me a lifetime 10 percent–off coupon on all Ralph Lauren products, although frankly, it would have to be closer to a 75 percent–off coupon before I could afford his goods.

But despite my concern for the good of mankind, I knew my mother would never understand. She had, after all, bought me a Chanel purse on their last trip to Iran, where, apparently, the people who stitched the tag were in a hurry and forgot the h, thus giving me the popular quilted "Canel" bag.

Six months and several dozen washes later, our comforter faded to a lighter shade of red, one that didn't quite scream "SOS" as loudly but just whimpered a faint "I'm an ugly knockoff." I finally decided that it was time to find *It* a new home. Sadly, this was not difficult, since San Francisco has many homeless residents. We didn't have to look far. There was a homeless woman with her dog who was a regular in our neighborhood. We handed her the comforter. She didn't react much, but from then on we could see her from blocks away.

François and I agreed that we wanted our next comforter to be blue and white, preferably with an Indian design. We decided to take our time finding just the right one, meanwhile enjoying the absence of *It*, which had taken our bedroom hostage for six months with its screaming color.

During my next phone conversation with my mother, I mentioned casually that the Ralph Lauren comforter had ceased to be. My mother was quite dismayed and wanted to know how I had washed it. I didn't want to say, "On the highest setting, every week," so I lied and said something about "Gentle cycle, cold water." The Inquisition continued. My mother asked me what kind of detergent I had used. I lied again and said, "Woolite," even pronouncing it "Voolite" to make the conversation flow more smoothly and possibly end sooner. My mother concluded that I had ruined the comforter. I apologized. She asked if Fransva was very disappointed. "Yes," I lied, again. My mother was very sad. I pretended to be sad, too. By then, with all my fibs, I knew that the devil himself was putting the finishing touches on a front-row-center seat in Hell, "Reserved for Firoozeh Dumas, Worst Daughter Ever."

A few months later, with the Iranian New Year approaching, my mother decided to visit us again. I cleaned the apartment thoroughly, even scrubbing the grout in the bathroom with a toothbrush. I bought her favorite kind of milk, the crunchy red apples she likes, and her preferred brand of tea. The hyacinths, part of the Iranian New Year tradition, were already on the table. I went to pick her up at the airport.

She stepped off the airplane laden with gifts: homemade baklava, *lavashak*, a sour fruit roll-up, pistachios, and of course, saffron that she had ground herself. She also had her usual fried eggplants with her so she would not waste any time making *khoresht-e bademjun*.

As we stood at the baggage claim, my mother brought me up to date on all the latest gossip in the family. Suddenly, midsentence, I saw, coming toward us on the luggage carousel, an enormous bright red package. It was like a mirage, except that mirages are illusions of things that one wishes existed. This was the opposite of a mirage.

I looked at my mother, who looked as if she were about to burst with joy. "I found another one!" she said. "I looked all over!"

This serve was not just an ace. This was an ace that ricocheted off the back wall and hit me in the head.

"I hated that comforter!" I blurted. "I can't believe you bought *another* one!" I said, somewhat loudly, forgetting I was in a public place.

My mother was shocked. "But Fransva loved it. You said you loved it, too," my mother added, looking completely dejected.

Meanwhile, the comforter had circled to where we were standing. I refused to pick it up.

"The reason I didn't tell you that I hated it is because I couldn't," I said, clenching my fists in frustration. "The way you set things up, it's not possible!" I whined.

"I don't understand," she said. "You said you loved it and Fransva loved it and it looked so good in your room."

"We hated it," I said. "We just said that. After all your stories of how hard you had looked to find something beautiful, we didn't have a choice. You left no room for us to tell you the truth."

In the meantime, the comforter had circled a few more times. Sadly, nobody had stolen it.

"What am I supposed to do?" my mother asked.

"Let's just leave it here," I suggested.

She looked at me as if I had suggested we rob a bank together.

"Nobody but you would say that to their mother," she said, looking away from me.

There was no winning this match.

I grabbed the comforter from the luggage carousel. "It stays in the car," I said.

My mother did not respond.

We drove home in silence. I tried to make small talk, but the guilt in the car was suffocating us.

"I'm very sorry," I said, at least four dozen times.

"But I brought this for Fransva," she said. "He lied to me, too?"

I had lost this tennis match and now the audience was throwing tomatoes at me.

"Actually, he liked it," I lied again, trying to cover up the truth.

"So why don't you keep it?" she asked meekly. "For Fransva."

"We'll do that," I said.

"And," she added, "this time, I found the sheets that go with it. We can surprise Fransva."

"Oh yes," I said, finally speaking the truth. "François *will* be surprised."

Doggie Don't

I live in a lovely neighborhood full of mature trees and well-maintained lawns. Like all desirable neighborhoods, home prices here leave prospective buyers wishing they had been born into a different family, more specifically, a rich one. Most couples, like my husband and I, dream of finding an affordable run-down property to renovate. After years of searching, we finally found a two-bedroom, one-bath fixer-upper near the railroad tracks. We considered ourselves very lucky, although we realized that when the realtor said, "You don't really hear the train," what he really meant is, "I want the commission from this sale."

The high point of the house was its garden. In the backyard, we planted trees and flowers that attracted butterflies and bees. In the front yard, we planted a Granny Smith tree, right in front of one of our large windows. I told my kids that since we did not have a TV, they could witness the four seasons on our apple tree. In addition, the tree attracted an endless number of squirrels, which are basically rats with really cute tails. These jittery creatures spent their days running up and down the branches, grabbing what food they could, and hastily eating it right in front of our window. "It's our own Animal Planet," I announced. My kids were young enough to be excited.

One morning, I opened the blinds as usual. My eyes immediately gravitated toward a small pyramid next to my apple tree. Somebody had allowed his dog to do what dogs do, on *our* lawn.

Not only are there laws against these types of gifts, but I could not help but take this personally. Why would somebody do this to us? Was this someone who knew us? Did this have something do with the increasing popularity of Persian cats?

I shared the news with my husband, who immediately went outside to investigate the evidence. "It's a medium-size dog," he surmised.

The next day, I opened the blinds and there, in the same place, was an almost identical mound. Twice in two days meant only one thing: there was a serial defecator on the loose.

My husband vowed to find the culprit.

I took matters into my own hands and bought an orange fluorescent posterboard, which I attached to the large oak in front of our sidewalk. "Please clean up after your dog! It's the law!" I wrote, making the exclamation points extra big to let everyone know I meant business.

My neighbors, too nice to tell me that my sign was probably bringing down real-estate prices, asked me how long I was planning to keep the sign up. "As long as I have to," I announced.

"This is happening either late at night or very early in the morning," my husband announced. "What we should do is keep our blinds open as late as possible and then wake up really early and open them."

Around the same time as this doggie caper, I had purchased red fleece pajamas from a catalog in Maine that specializes in practical, comfortable, and somewhat ugly clothing. I had purchased the pajamas not for aesthetics, but for the simple reason that I turn into a cold-blooded reptile at night. Granted, they were not the most feminine items, more Margaret Thatcher than Sophia Loren, but then again my Victoria's Secret catalog always seems to be missing the "Comfortable and Practical" section. My husband hated my pajamas and referred to them as "the Santa suit," to which I always replied, "Ho, ho, ho."

Every morning, I opened the blinds and surveyed the people walking outside. I noticed that in my neighborhood, there was an abundance of people walking their dogs in the mornings, but most people had either small breeds (or non-dogs, as they are known in our household) or large ones. There was a strange lack of medium-size dogs, which further increased the mystery.

In retrospect, I may have been a bit obsessive, but there is something about cleaning up somebody else's doggie doo that brings out the worst in humanity, or at least in me. Despite my attempts to outsmart the dog, the canine culprit succeeded in leaving several more pyramids.

Finally, one morning, my vigilance paid off. I spotted a woman walking not one but two medium-size dogs. The dogs were unruly, the kind who would do their deed wherever they desired, regardless of whatever commands their owner might yell. These dogs looked guilty. I opened my front door, still wearing the Santa suit, put my hands on my hips, and glared at the owner. She looked at me and continued on her way.

The next morning, the same woman appeared, walking the same defiant medium-size dogs. The dogs looked guiltier than the day before. I once again opened the front door, walked outside, and glared at the woman.

This was the first time I had used the Look of Death Glaring Technique, ever. As a nonconfrontational type, I have to consciously practice *not* apologizing when someone bumps into me. This was a huge milestone for me. I could now effectively get a job in a Parisian café.

My husband thought I was taking this too far. "You have never witnessed these dogs even walking on our lawn. Maybe you should tone it down a bit." It was too late. The power I felt in the red fleece suit, combined with the hands on the hips, had turned me into a suburban superhero, Super Bitch.

After a week of glaring at this woman, I noticed that when she got to my house, she actually crossed the street *to avoid me.* I could hear the trumpets playing my victory song.

About a month later, our local paper announced that the elementary school where my children attended had finally found a new principal. I looked at the picture of the new principal and knew that I had seen her somewhere but could not remember where.

The next morning I opened the blinds, and it suddenly hit me like a ton of bricks, or in this case, excrement. There was the new principal, walking her two medium-size dogs, which suddenly no longer looked guilty at all. In fact, they looked cute. I ran outside, in the Santa suit, hands no longer on my hips, and approached her as gently as I could, given the fact that I had spent the past week glaring at her.

"Hello! Are you the new principal?" I asked.

"Yes, I am," she answered.

"Nice to meet you," I said. "You see, we were having problems with a dog leaving stuff on our lawn but I know they weren't your dogs."

"Nice to meet you, too," she said.

After that verbal exchange, I looked forward to many more years of awkward conversations with my children's principal. I had no choice but to pretend none of it had ever happened. To aid my denial of the events, I got rid of the fleece pajamas. The Frenchman was delighted. I also had to forgive myself for my ugly behavior, which wasn't quite as easy as getting rid of ugly sleepwear. I did, however, sign up to make cupcakes for the teachers' lounge.

Mohammad, Kazem,
Nematollah, and Bob

Retirement does funny things to people. Take my father and his two brothers. Now that the three of them are no longer burdened by the demands of their respective engineering and medical careers, they somehow have to fill up the time previously spent building oil refineries and healing the sick.

Every weekday morning, the three of them meet at my uncle Nematollah's house at a quarter to ten. Why at Uncle Nematollah's and not at Uncle Mohammad's or my dad's? Because Uncle Nematollah owns a coffeemaker.

The three of them grab their coffees. My father complains that the coffee is cheap. My uncle Nematollah tells him that he would never know the difference between expensive and cheap coffee, so why should he waste the money? Then the three of them head to a room in the back of the house. They shut the door. They turn on the TV.

It's time.

It's time for *The Price Is Right.*

I found out about this ritual the same way that penicillin or chocolate chip cookies were discovered, by accident.

Every time I fly to see my parents, I book the flight that arrives at 10:30 AM. I have always assumed that this is a convenient time for my eighty-year-old father to pick me up at the airport, a ten-minute drive from his house. My parents always seem genuinely happy to see me. I do, however, sense a palpable resentment from my uncle Nematollah, who regularly asks me, "Weren't you just here?"

He finally let the Persian cat out of the bag one day. "Can't you take a later flight?" he asked. "Why?" I wanted to know. He refused to tell me. I insisted. And that's how I stumbled upon their little secret.

I agreed to come at a different time. "But first," I said, "you must let me watch." This was not met with enthusiasm.

The very next day I, too, was in the back room of my uncle Nematollah's house. The three of them were talking at the same time, like they always do. Then the game show's theme music started. The conversation immediately stopped.

The commentary started as soon as the first contestant was told to "come on down!"

"She's going to be a screamer. She'd better not win."

"You think he could wear something nicer than shorts on TV."

"I'm rooting for him. Doesn't he remind you of Hassani?"

The Price Is Right is based essentially on the ability to guess the price of a ceiling fan or a case of men's hair color. For the average viewer, the show does not reveal much about the character of each contestant. But like the college students who somehow managed to turn *The Bob Newhart Show* into a drinking game, my father and his brothers have taken the show to a whole new level. They interpret every squeal, every jump, every guess as a window into the character of each contestant, thereby allowing them to decide who deserves to win and, more important, who doesn't. For them, it's not simply a show about people wearing T-shirts declaring "Happy Birthday to my sister Wanda!" on national television while jumping up and down at the prospect of winning a cumbersome bedroom set for which they have no room. It's a show that allows the three brothers to act as God, while wielding no real power whatsoever.

"I don't know why any of you cares who wins since it doesn't affect any of you anyway," I said.

There was no comment.

The first item for bid that day was a Jet Ski. None of the four people bidding looked like they had ever operated one. They looked like types who would hurt themselves on Jet Skis. Nonetheless, they all jumped and squealed while the audience shouted out seemingly random numbers, since how many people have ever actually purchased a Jet Ski? Much to the horror of my father and uncles, the loudest contestant won. As she bunny-hopped to the stage to kiss Bob Barker, she kept looking back at the audience to her equally loud cheering section.

"*Khoda be dod-e ma bereseh.* God help us," said my uncle Mohammad.

"The worst part," I said, "is that they have to pay taxes on the prizes, so not only are they stuck with something they don't need, but they have to partially pay for it. Nothing's free," I added, trying to add a layer of education to our activity.

"By the way, you're not invited again," my uncle Nematollah said.

"Why?" I asked.

"You talk too much."

The final portion of the program, the Showcase Showdown, arrived. That's when the prizes move beyond coffee-makers and a year's supply of macaroni and cheese to cars and vacations. And that's when the brothers all started shouting out numbers at the TV screen.

"Twenty-two thousand!" my father yelled, pointing his finger at Bob Barker, expecting a personal nod back.

"Forty-five thousand," added my eighty-six-year-old uncle Mohammad.

"How much is an RV?" Nematollah asked.

The contestant who won bid one dollar. This devious tactic assumes that the other contestant will overbid. It worked. The brothers were angry. They didn't like the woman who won. She was The Screamer.

"No dignity," they said, looking genuinely disappointed. "None at all."

Last year, my uncle Nematollah had surgery. When he came home from the hospital, he was feeling weak and didn't want any visitors. We were all worried about him. No one could remember a time when he didn't want visitors.

A week later, he called his brothers and invited them to his house at 9:45 AM. "Don't be late," he said.

They weren't.

Seyyed Abdullah Jazayeri

When my mother called to tell me that my uncle Abdullah had passed away, I wasn't surprised. The last time I had seen him, he was a shadow of his former self, bedridden and dependent on others for all his needs. He had spent the last few months of his life in a rented hospital bed in the living room of his condominium in Southern California. Outside the window, he could see the fruit trees he and my aunt Sedigeh had planted to remind them of Iran. Their green thumbs had defied space limitations. In their tiny yard they had not only an enormous fig tree but also a sweet lemon tree (a *naranj,* which is a cross between an orange and a lemon), a pomegranate tree, and a row of cypresses that resembled the backdrops in Persian miniatures. Their fruit trees were famous for bearing more fruit than anybody else's, undoubtedly to accommodate my aunt Sedigeh's generous nature. During fig season, my father visited my uncle Abdullah and aunt Sedigeh every day.

While my uncle Abdullah lay on his bed, visitors streamed in all day. His sons, their wives, their children, and their children's children all altered their schedules every day to be with him. Uncle Abdullah's son Mehdi and his daughter-in-law Mary flew from Italy several times, their son Darius came from Rwanda, my cousin Ryan from New York. Others spent hours on the L.A. freeway to visit Uncle Abdullah, which for anyone familiar with L.A. freeways, is almost as impressive as coming from Rwanda.

My uncle died surrounded by his loved ones, his garden, his books, and more framed photos of his family than any decorator would allow in one room. For a man whose mother died soon after childbirth, permanently depriving him of a mother's love, there could not have been a gentler, more embraced departure.

A few days after his passing, I received a phone call from my cousin Mahmood announcing that instead of the usual somber memorial, the family had decided to have a "celebration of life." To my American sensibility, this seemed appropriate. My uncle had lived a very full life; his death was not unexpected. Not all deaths can be marked with a celebration of life, but if anyone's could, it would be my uncle's. I was, however, highly skeptical that my Iranian family would pull this off.

If there's one thing that separates Middle Easterners from Westerners, it's the way we mourn. We can out-mourn anyone. For many in the Middle East, a highly emotional funeral is proof that the deceased is missed. Jackie Kennedy's stoicism after the death of her husband would not have translated well in the Middle East. In Iran, there is something called *tabaki*,

which is the act of attending funerals and other religious cere-
monies such as *rozeh khooni* to cry and encourage others to
follow suit. It is considered a good deed to help others release
their pain. One can also hire professional mourners, who re-
cite prayers from the Koran and encourage everyone to cry. In
Tabaki, a fascinating documentary about the world of professional mourners, Iranian filmmaker Bahman Kiarostami inter-
views many in the field, who discuss their unique calling and
their previous jobs—one worked in airport security, another
was a welder, but each had decided to take up this second
profession. Living in an Islamic theocracy, there is a market
for such services, sort of like people in America obtaining real-
estate licenses to take advantage of hot real-estate markets.

In Iranian culture, we mourn the day a loved one passes,
the day he is buried, three days after, seven days after, forty
days after, and at the one-year mark. After that, we mourn
every year the day of the passing. People often visit the grave
site of a loved one at the end of every week.

In the United States, the ability to "move on" after a death
is usually seen as a sign of inner strength and generally com-
mended. A widow who starts dating is often called a survivor.
In Middle Eastern culture, however, a widow who starts
openly dating is looked upon with suspicion and disdain. A
widow who mourns her husband for the rest of her life is
viewed as devoted. Of course no one expects a widower to
stay single his whole life, but that's a whole other book.

An American friend of mine lost her father a month before
her wedding. She told me that even though she considered
canceling the wedding, her family urged her to go on, knowing that her father would have wanted it that way. In Iranian
culture, that family would have been saying sayonara to their
wedding deposits. The couple might go off and get married

quietly, but there would certainly be no reception, music, or dancing. It would be unimaginable to have any celebration so close to the death of a parent.

When Mahmood told me about the intended "celebration of life" for his father, I realized how much my family had quietly changed by living in America. Unlike playing dodgeball, this was one part of American culture that I could wholeheartedly embrace.

To complicate matters, my cousin Mahmood asked me to speak at the "celebration." I was not sure how honest my culture would allow me to be at such a traditional ceremony. To stay true to my uncle's memory, I would have to share some of the stories about him that always made me laugh, but that just seemed too American for my family.

When I think of my uncle Abdullah, I think of a man whom I loved deeply. He was the first person I ever met who loved words and the only person in my family who had shelves and shelves of books. His attention to detail was legendary, as was his talent for giving really long answers to just about any question. This aspect of his personality was even evident in his verbose answering machine message in America: my uncle's voice, enunciating every syllable, giving long, detailed instructions, in Persian, exactly how to respond to the "beep," a word that he pronounced with a distinct Persian accent.

From the time I was a little girl in Abadan to the time I had my own children, Uncle Abdullah was always happy to see me, as I was to see him. And he always said that I was the one person he knew who had never changed. I thought the same thing about him. I always laughed at his jokes, even though they were usually at the expense of my father. My father laughed, too.

But I also remember my uncle as someone with a severe case of directional dyslexia. I think of a man who set out one day to drive one hour north to Los Angeles and instead drove two hours south to Mexico. This unexpected visit to our neighbor to the south happened while my cousin Fakhri, Uncle Abdullah's hapless passenger, repeatedly said, "Uncle Abdullah, this doesn't look right." Not until they reached the Bienvenidos a Mexico! sign did my uncle acknowledge his mistake, at which point, he calmly turned around and drove the other way.

In Iranian culture, this is not the type of story one shares at a memorial service.

The service was held in the conference room of a local hotel. Enormous floral arrangements filled the room. The event started with my cousin Mahmood recounting his father's personal and professional achievements. This is what we all expected. Six hundred people dressed in black listened quietly as my cousin recounted the life of his father from his humble beginnings in the south of Iran to his life in California. Some sobbed quietly. Then my cousin told the audience that his father, at age seventy, had decided to learn to play the flute. I assumed this story would highlight my uncle's endless love of learning. Instead, my cousin told us that although his father lacked musical talent, he kept practicing. He practiced so much and so badly that the condominium association asked him to stop.

And that is when I heard something that I never thought I would hear at an Iranian memorial service: laughter, albeit tentative laughter.

My uncle's grandson, Peter, né Farbod, got up to speak next. He and his American wife, Julie, née Julie, had put together a slide show of my uncle's life, set to Beatles music: the stern wedding portrait showing him and my aunt far too young to be getting married; still baby-faced but now holding their own babies; images of trips to the Caspian Sea with their sons, all knobby knees and spindly arms; Mahmood on a wobbly tricycle; weddings with smiling daughters-in-law, the same ones who had held Uncle Abdullah's hand for the past six months; grandchildren of all ages, each one of them knowing what it's like to be loved; snapshots of everyone in Hawaii wearing leis, wrinkle-free faces not fully appreciated at the time; college graduations of those long-ago babies; more wrinkled faces; my aunt and uncle all dressed up in front of the Stardust in Las Vegas with smiles that said, "It's a long way from Abadan!"; my uncle wearing seventies sunglasses, long sideburns, and more wrinkles; and finally the photos taken during the last year, his body looking frail and tired, knowing the end is near but still smiling, testimony that where we begin does not determine where we end. Ninety years of my uncle's life in fifteen minutes. Tears flowed as Paul McCartney's voice filled the room.

My cousin Mehdi, my uncle's third son, got up to speak but he couldn't. He was crying. After a few awkward minutes, he told a few stories about what a loving father and grandfather my uncle had been. He told us about my uncle's unending devotion to his children and grandchildren. Then he told the audience that his father had missed the birth of his son because he got lost on the way to the hospital. Everyone laughed. Mehdi told us that they had practiced driving to the hospital half a dozen times with his father because he had a tendency to get lost. But he *still* got lost. The audience roared. I couldn't believe my ears.

Looking around me, I realized that my uncle should have written a book. How had he and my aunt raised four decent, successful sons who married women who completed them? How had they ended up with seven grandchildren, each of them kind, bright, and book lovers to boot, the kind of children who go out of their way to have conversations with elderly relatives, even if those conversations start with "Shouldn't you be married by now?"

My uncle was too busy reading ever to write his own stories. He was never without a book, and everyone knew that lending him any book meant kissing that book goodbye for at least a year, sometimes three in the case of *Gorky Park* or anything by James Michener. My uncle was one of the few people I knew who looked up every word he didn't know. He then wrote down those words in a notebook and asked others if they knew them. This habit did not give him the best reputation for scintillating party conversation, but I found it quite endearing. Had he not been born poor in Iran so long ago, I imagine he would have become an English professor, or at least a spelling bee champ.

When it was my turn to speak, I shared a few stories about my uncle's quirky personality and his endearing love for his family. I ended my eulogy by saying that even though Uncle Abdullah was frequently lost on the freeways, in life, he knew exactly which road to take. His inner GPS worked just fine. Everyone agreed.

My uncle, along with the rest of my family, came to America seeking a better life. Like so many immigrants before us, we found not only what we wanted but a few things we didn't even know we were looking for: Girl Scouts, freedom of speech, affordable community colleges, guacamole, public libraries, clean bathrooms, the pursuit of happiness, and Loehmann's. Of course we also found a few things we didn't like: marshmallows, the Hilton sisters and all their friends, the lack of interest in geography, those pants that ride way too low, and tomatoes that taste like cardboard. Regardless of the influences, we swore we would live in this country but never change. We were wrong. America changed us, in ways we didn't realize. Oddly enough, we also changed America. We expanded the palates of many friends to include *tadig, joojeh kabob,* and desserts made with rose water. Any American who has attended a Persian wedding knows that dancing is not limited by age, weight, or ability, and yes, it's okay for men to dance in ways that John Wayne wouldn't. And if there's one thing I hope we Iranians have imparted, it is the closeness of extended family, not because we all get along perfectly, but because we know that we all benefit emotionally from maintaining those ties. Our parents often do live with us in their twilight years, and yes, they get on our nerves. In fact, our mothers only meddle *more* as they get older. Some things don't change.

Those parts of our lives that changed were not what we expected. Who knew that someday we would wear leg warmers and take aerobics classes? We knew we wanted our family members to become educated but who knew that we'd forget some of our Persian and pick up some Spanish? We wanted to have comfortable lives and the right to vote. Who would ever have guessed that someday we would be voting for Iranian candidates running for office in America, candidates who actually won? We wanted to pursue lives well lived. Who knew that someday we would allow ourselves to remember those lives in a whole new way, with smiles, laughter, and Beatles music? We may never put ice in our tea, but we can, when appropriate, celebrate the lives of loved ones, even if it's not the way we normally do things. That, perhaps more than all the other changes, feels downright revolutionary. I'm sure my uncle Abdullah would agree.

Encore, Unfortunately

Some things, like the eighties, should never come back.

It all started in 1979, which to borrow the words of Queen Elizabeth II, was my "annus horribilis." My father, who had worked for the same company his whole life, lost his job. My mother decided she was now from "Torekey," and Americans decided it was time for us to go home.

It all happened so fast. It seemed like on Monday, everyone was asking us if our carpets really do fly. Then on Friday, those same people were putting "I Play Cowboys and Iranians" bumper stickers on their cars. I was fourteen, and all this sudden hatred really got me thinking. What type of person would make bumper stickers announcing hatred? Who would buy one of those bumper stickers and actually put it on his car? Isn't that the type of feeling people ideally should not have or, if they do, should at least keep private? Every time I saw one of those bumper stickers, and there were plenty, I tried to get a look at the driver. I don't remember what any of them looked like. I do remember my heart beating fast.

Then there was the song "Bomb Iran," sung to the tune of the Beach Boys song "Barbara Ann." It had this terrible chorus that stuck in your head like the ba-ra-ba-bum-bum of "The Little Drummer Boy." Disc jockeys loved "Bomb Iran," and made it one of the top hits of 1980. They played it over and over and over again. It was the soundtrack to all my nightmares.

Fast-forward twenty-five years: I needed to get a copy of the "Bomb Iran" song for my one-woman show about growing up Iranian in America. Thanks to the Internet, I found Vince Vance and the Valiants' website. There were phone numbers listed for Georgia, Louisiana, Mississippi, and Texas. I randomly dialed one of the numbers. A woman answered.

"Vince Vance and the Valiants Fan Club," she said.

I told her I needed a copy of "Bomb Iran." I even pronounced Iran "I-Ran," even though it's supposed to be pronounced "Ee-ron." This wasn't the moment to be educational.

"We don't have it," the woman said.

"I'm Iranian and I have a one-woman show and I *really* need that soundtrack. Can you please help me find it?"

There was a long pause. "You're I-raynian and you want a copy of 'Bomb I-Ran'?" she asked, sounding rather startled.

"Yes," I said.

"Hold on, please," she replied.

Then I heard muffled sounds and a man picked up the phone.

"Is this Vince?" I asked.

"Yes, it is," the man said.

Then the conversation took a strange turn. He started apologizing.

"What's your name?" he asked. Then he earnestly tried to pronounce it.

"I didn't mean anything by that song," he said. "I had no idea it would take off like that." He told me that his manager had suggested he write parodies, and that the song was addressed to the Ayatollah, not to the people of Iran. He was stunned by its success. Carter's rescue mission had failed, and Americans felt humiliated. Speaking like a true poet, he said it was "like a pimple that erupted." He said that one time, the KKK showed up at one of his concerts to support him. "That was awful," he added.

He sent me the lyrics of the song by e-mail, plus another apology. He quoted Keats. He sent me pictures of himself with his signature eighteen-inch hairdo. He invited me to one of his performances. I told him that if my show was picked up for the season, I would make sure he received royalties. "Don't worry about that," he said. "You won't make any money."

"Bomb Iran" recently came back, thanks to John McCain, who sang part of it during one of his speeches. I called Vince (real name Andrew Franichevich), to see what he thought. He didn't return my call. Maybe he was too busy. He is, after all, a very successful guy. Or maybe he is a bit horrified like I was, that the song, like a disease that we think has been eradicated, was back.

Last Mango in Paris

The Japanese have a saying that for every new food we try, we gain seven days of life. I may be immortal by now. The realm of gastronomy represents the only area where I deliberately seek adventure. I'll try *almost* anything. I live by the "One bite won't kill you" rule, and know that no flavor, however revolting, will linger forever, especially when followed by enough water. I have also learned that one country's gourmet fare is another country's cat food, and oftentimes the impression we make at someone else's dining table determines the course of the relationship. Needless to say, many of my friendships were forged around a meal.

For most cultures, food is the glue that binds. It doesn't matter if what you are being served tastes like glue; you have to eat it. In Iranian culture, there is no bigger insult than to refuse to try a food prepared by your host. You will make a really bad impression that, short of your curing cancer or bringing peace to the Middle East, will never go away. And if you're ever lucky enough to be invited to an Iranian's home, you never have to worry about weird food, since we use only beef, lamb, fish, and chicken. You will probably end up trying new herbs and spices, maybe tamarind or fenugreek, but if that scares you, then you should get started on that cancer cure now.

Growing up in Iran, I had access only to Persian food, which is surprisingly varied. Even though Iran is a very small country compared to the United States, its cuisine is endless thanks to its abundance of fruits, vegetables, and herbs. Most Westerners envisage only a desert when imagining Iran, which is one of the many reasons why geography should be brought back to American classrooms. Iran's climate varies from north to south, east to west. Even though Iran does have a desert, it also has snow, subtropical climates, and abundant gardens. Some archaeologists even believe Iran is the location of the Garden of Eden.

Iran's climatic variations have resulted in an abundance of natural gifts. Peaches, almonds, persimmons, and pomegranates are just a few of the plants indigenous to Iran. Even tulips, which everyone associates with Holland, are native to Iran, Afghanistan, and Central Asia.

Given the country's cornucopia of riches, every region in Iran has its own culinary specialties, ranging from my favorite *mirza ghasemi,* an eggplant dish of the north, to *ghalyeh mahi,* a fish stew containing tamarind, of the south. Iranians have been very adept at incorporating local ingredients in their cuisine, making traveling in Iran a true adventure for the gourmand.

But even the most devoted gourmand will tell you that

every country's cuisine has a few strange, perhaps even revolting, dishes, the types of food that leave the average American guest suddenly remembering that he left his stove on and has to rush home. Sometimes these dishes consist of animals normally kept as pets in one's native culture, but served on a plate in others. Dogs and rats, consumed in parts of Southeast Asia, come to mind. Then there are parts of animals not normally consumed in this country by humans or other species. Bovine urine, reputedly drunk by the Maasai, is a good example. The old saying that we shouldn't judge someone without walking in their boots would be difficult in the case of the Maasai, who are famously known for walking barefoot. Although it would take one heck of a marketing campaign to sell bovine urine in the West, who's to say it's any stranger than the chemical cocktail known as diet soda? Judging by the number of overweight people who religiously consume massive amounts of diet drinks, a Martian might assume that it is a rather fattening concoction. The Maasai, on the other hand, all look like runway models. Perhaps marketing bovine urine in the United States would not be that difficult after all.

The topic of strange foods would never be complete without two words that should never go together, "maggot cheese." This delicacy from Sardinia reminds us of the elasticity of the word "delicacy." Most Americans would never consider eating insects unless it involved a TV show and a million-dollar prize. A connoisseur of insects, however, once told me that shrimp, which I eat, are nothing more than roaches of the sea. "It's all how you look at it," he said. "Shrimp and roaches, both arthropods, serve the same purpose in our ecological system. One is underwater, the other on land." His argument made sense, but I will wait until my favorite Chinese restaurant, Jing Jing, serves Kung Pao Roach to pass judgment.

Most cultures believe that once an animal is killed, nothing of it should be wasted. I completely agree with this. Knowing this has at least justified the existence of some strange foods, such as the plates of chicken feet I face whenever I go out for dim sum. It is from this noble philosophy that some of the stranger foods in my own culture are born.

As a child, I used to love fried sheep's brain. I knew that it was called *maghz,* or brain, but I thought it was because it *looked* like brains, sort of like big cauliflowers. It never occurred to me that the dish called "brains" actually was brains. Once I found out that it was what it was called, I no longer ate it.

Another popular specialty is tongue stew. I have never tried this dish because my mother, in her only feminist stand against my father, refused to cook it. None of my aunts ever prepared it, either. The only time I was ever served tongue was while flying alone on an Iran Air flight from Switzerland to Iran. I opened the sandwich to see what sort of meat it contained and realized that somewhere, a cow was missing its tongue. I was twelve years old and the sight of that cold, folded-up tongue completely killed my appetite all the way to Iran.

The hands-down winner in the category of Persian food that guarantees your American guests will never come to your house again is *kaleh pacheh,* sheep's head and feet soup. This recipe requires the purchase of an entire mutton or lamb's head, which is much harder to find than, say, a head of lettuce. Assuming one manages to obtain the aforementioned animal head, one must first burn the hairs off of it over an open flame. The cook should, at this point, receive a Girl Scout badge. She must then *remove the nose.* I can think of no other recipe with those three words but such is the charm of international cuisine. Then there's the matter of splitting the head, cooking it, and serving it to guests, all of whom should know what is coming their way. Serving *kaleh pacheh* to an unsuspecting guest should be categorized as a crime.

The only person in my extended family devoted to *kaleh pacheh* is my uncle Mohammad. He has been known to drive to his favorite *kaleh pacheh* restaurant to eat this delicacy for breakfast, which is the common practice. The only upside to starting the day eating a sheep's head is knowing that no matter how bad a day you may have, it won't be as bad as the sheep's.

Americans often claim that there is nothing "weird" in American cuisine. Oh, the sweet naïveté of that statement! Everybody thinks that about his own culture. Whatever one grows up with is normal. It's what the *other* guy is eating that is "weird."

When we first came to America, our enthusiasm for this culture was evident in our desire to try every single American food. Obviously this style of adventurism has a downside, but thanks to stretchy polyester clothing, we were able to forge ahead.

The strangest food for me, initially, was peanut butter. Its consistency was unlike anything I had ever tasted. It made me think of spackle. It wasn't until I tasted peanut butter with chocolate that I became a convert. My devotion has never wavered.

My least favorite American food, then and now, is frosting. The first time I tried it was in second grade, during a class birthday celebration. One of the moms came to class carrying a trayful of cute little cupcakes with a mountain of blue frosting on each. The frosting looked good, but looks are deceiving. One bite and I felt like someone had hit me over the head with a hammer. It was unbearably sweet. I could not eat it, but was concerned about appearing rude. I didn't know that in America, people are not offended if you don't eat their food. I pretended to eat it but instead discreetly squished the cupcake in my napkin and hid it in my pocket. My mom found it a week later, led there by the army of ants invading my room.

In general, I find that American desserts tend to be overly sweet. It's as if the point is to overwhelm the senses with sweetness, drowning all other flavors and leaving no room for subtlety. It's like listening to a band where one hears only the drums.

The weirdest American culinary marriage is yams with melted marshmallows. I don't know who thought of this Thanksgiving tradition but I'm guessing a hyperactive, toothless three-year-old. I just don't understand this random pairing. It's like Einstein marrying Charo. Yams are perfect plain. Dressing them up is like putting makeup on a ten-year-old girl or on Albert Einstein. It's just wrong and unnecessary.

My final gripe is with a food that I have never tried. I know that one cannot claim to dislike a food without having tried several versions of it, but in this case I make an exception. From my Iranian palate, the single most disgusting American creation is pork rinds. And no, this has nothing to do with my being Muslim. I like a ham and cheese sandwich as much as any descendant of the *Mayflower,* but deep fried pork skins sound inappropriate for human consumption. I'm sure they wouldn't be healthy for pets or plants, either, so maybe pork rinds should be fed to species we are trying to get rid of, such as maggots—but not in Sardinia.

My favorite American foods are sushi and guacamole, although not together. Whenever I travel, I insist on eating the local cuisine so I can learn something about the people. That's a noble excuse, and it sounds a lot better than "I like to eat."

Ironically, most people want to invite me to the one Middle Eastern restaurant in town, or else I get a homemade Persian meal, but an always unique version. This meal is usually preceded with an explanation: "Our English teacher's husband was in the Peace Corps in Namibia. He also traveled to Turkey once. He has volunteered to cook a Persian dinner from recipes he found on the Internet." Whatever these meals may lack in authenticity, they more than make up for in generosity and kindness.

I have also had many memorable local meals while traveling. I have added egg salad sandwiches in New York, Maryland crab, Smith Island cake, pork tenderloin sandwiches in Iowa, and lobster rolls from Gloucester (*lobstah* from *Gloustah*) to my roster of favorites. The list keeps growing, and that's a very good thing.

When I married a Frenchman, my palate widened even further. Thanks to François, I tried stuffed quail and pâté, regional wines and endless stinky but delicious cheeses. I loved French food and found myself becoming more and more adventurous every time we visited his country. But like the skydiver who eventually lands on his head and decides that maybe it's time to redirect his bravery, I, too, found myself redirected, toward the vegetarian menu.

It all started years ago when my husband and I discovered a charming little restaurant in an alley in the seventh arrondissement in Paris. This tiny restaurant, with its red gingham curtains and only nine tables, opened every day at noon to a line of hungry Parisians waiting outside calmly and quietly. Complete strangers were forced to eat at the same table, and people were often asked to change tables in the middle of a meal if the lack of seating necessitated such choreography. Nobody ever complained. The food was so good that a little bit of abuse seemed a small price to pay for a perfect *coq au vin*. What was most surprising were the prices. This place was actually cheap. A three-course meal, complete with a glass of wine, was about ten dollars. (The prices have since changed.)

During one of our excursions, our son ordered a salmon dish, which he did not like. This was a first for us, but then again, our son was four. When we tried to order dessert, the waitress, who was the chef's wife, told us that there would be no dessert until the salmon was finished. "*Ca ennuyera le chef.* That will bother the chef," she told us. In America, this bold gesture would have seemed pushy and inappropriate, but bathed in French light, it seemed charming, a bit like the sign in our elevator that read, "*Ne pas cracher.*" Do not spit.

We go to France only about once every five years, so when we found ourselves in France again last Christmas, we were thrilled. Our children were ten and thirteen, young enough to still want to hang out with their parents but old enough to have strong bladders. With the dearth of public bathrooms abroad, the latter is appreciated only if one has traveled with a toddler.

Having an Iranian mother and a French father, my children have been taught that trying new foods is a necessary and exciting part of life. They have to have only one bite but are never, ever, under any circumstances, allowed to make a face or say "oooh" or "yuck." If they don't like something, "no, thank you" are the operative words.

During our last excursion to Paris, we took the children to our usual little bistro. The specialty that day was *andouillette,* a type of sausage. None of us, the Frenchman included, were clear on what exactly went in *andouillette,* but then again, as the saying goes, the exact ingredients of any sausage are known only to the sausage maker and God. Plus, we didn't care what was in it; we were in France and that meant that we could not go wrong. My husband and daughter ordered it; my son and I ordered different dishes so we could all share.

As we waited anxiously for our food, my husband and I enjoyed a glass of Côte du Ventoux, a red wine from the south of France. Our children were busy with the baguette and butter, a simple but sublime combination the French have perfected. Our appetizers arrived: leeks vinaigrette (the white part of the leek, boiled, cooled, then served with a creamy vinaigrette).

All of a sudden, my son started looking around the restaurant. Something smelled funny.

Our main course was arriving.

The *andouillette* looked like fat, pale sausage. My husband and daughter each took a bite and said nothing. I noticed that the portion size was rather large, so I told my ten-year-old daughter, "Leave half of it. It's too much." Normally, the suggestion of eating only half a dish is a cause for protest from my daughter. This time, she agreed without any argument. That should have been a clue.

I asked my daughter if I could taste the sausage. "Sure," she said, giving me a generous serving. Her generosity should have been my second clue.

I took a bite. I couldn't taste anything. My palate was overwhelmed with something I could not identify.

This is the point where good judgment flew out the window. Rather than give my palate time to reach within its Rolodex of previous taste experiences, I decided to speed the process by taking another bite. With the second bite in my mouth, I still could not identify the flavors, except that I felt that I was eating something not meant to be eaten.

My thirteen-year-old had also taken a bite of *andouillette* and was now gulping down several glasses of water. "That's the most disgusting thing I have ever tasted," he declared. Normally, I would say something like "It's enough to say you don't like it," except that his words were utterly true. My daughter added, "I can't finish this." My husband was turning *vert.*

It wasn't just the flavor but the fact that it lingered regardless of the amount of fluid we consumed. Even though none of us had eaten more than a few bites, it felt like a brick had found its way into our gut. If only life came with Rewind and Delete buttons.

"What is in this?" I asked the French husband. He didn't know. We asked the waitress, who proceeded to give us a long list of ingredients, but all I heard was "pig intestines."

The waitress was not happy when we told her that we could not eat any more, but there was no option here. Short of Moses appearing and commanding us to finish the *andouillette,* we wouldn't.

We paid the bill, which was more than a hundred dollars, thus adding another level of horror to our experience. As we staggered to the nearby Metro station, all we could talk about was the taste-and-smell combination that had left a permanent imprint on our brains. We desperately devoured the Altoids I had brought from the United States, but Altoids were no match for the potency of the *andouillette.* It was as if the flavor had penetrated our teeth's dentin. We spent the rest of the afternoon brushing, flossing, and rinsing, then repeating.

That night, we went to dinner at my in-laws'. When we explained why we all felt sick and wouldn't be able to eat, my mother-in-law asked if the *andouillette* had smelled bad, sort of like a toilet. "Yes," we said. "Then the intestines had not been cleaned well," she casually explained.

We didn't think it was possible to feel any worse after that meal, but now we did. I decided I needed more information. Maybe my mother-in-law was wrong. Maybe the latrine smell was a result of a mélange of secret French spices.

The next day, I went to the local butcher and asked him how one prepares *andouillette*.

"Il faut d'abord bien nettoyer le debris," he said. "You must first thoroughly remove the particles."

On my way home, I swore off all sausage forever. I regretted asking the butcher for more information. I regretted having learned French so that I could ask the butcher for more information. From now on, I told myself, I will stick to foods I know. In fact, I will stick to foods that grow on trees. And when I want adventure, I will go to a Barry Manilow concert.

And that is when I saw a small mound of perfectly ripe mangos in the window of an exclusive *epicerie*. Here was an example of a perfect food. I looked at the price and knew that if my father ever found out how much I was contemplating on spending on a single mango, his frugal immigrant's sensibility would be horrified. But then again, if he knew what was in the lunch I had eaten, he would be even more horrified.

I bought the mango and did what no self-respecting French person would ever do. I sat on a nearby bench, took out my Swiss army knife, and ate it right then and there. With every bite, its ripe, succulent flesh erased the memory of my gastronomical misadventure. My senses were mesmerized by its natural sweetness. The best part was that my mango contained no pork parts, frosting, or marshmallows. All I could taste was its perfection, courtesy of nature. I threw the pit in the nearby wastebasket and wiped the juice from my chin.

And then the taste of the *andouillette* came back to me.

Mr. Potato

I have always been destined to be rich. This I know for sure because put me in any store, be it a tile, shoe, or pet shop, and I will gravitate toward the most expensive item. I do this effortlessly, like someone possessing an inner dowsing stick or divining rod.

The problem is that the universe has not yet caught up with my destiny, but that's part of the plan, too. It's better to achieve success later and have it be real than to become famous and have it taken away. Just ask the former planet Pluto. But I have always known that someday something would happen and I would be suddenly rich, and not like one of those people who saves a hundred dollars every month and *eventually* becomes rich. My good fortune would be more akin to the guy who invented Post-its. One good idea and you never again have to ask, "How much is that puppy in the window?"

While I await that day, I enjoy the many fine things in life that are free, my favorite being going to the farmers market. It's like a religious experience, and I am forever preaching its value. I regularly buy gifts for friends there, such as a spectacular bunch of radishes or a stick of brussels sprouts that looks like a medieval weapon. One time I bought a huge striped cucumber shaped like an *S*. The recipient of this gift, a five-year-old, was thrilled. On rainy days, I thank all the farmers for coming and buy twice as much.

One day I was at the market as usual, looking through the organic fingerling potatoes, and suddenly there it was, a perfect cross-shaped potato. I mean perfect. I showed it to the woman next to me, who looked impressed and then asked me if I knew where to find lemon basil. This is probably what happened to the guy who invented the Hula Hoop. He showed it to his wife, who reminded him not to forget to put out the trash. But I knew what I had.

I came home and showed the potato to the French husband, who thought it was "cute." But my thirteen-year-old got it right away. "EBay!" he yelled. We all know the story of the guy who sold a piece of toast on eBay that supposedly had an image of the Virgin Mary on it. This would be the sequel.

Problem was, I did not want to insult anyone. How do I list something like this for sale without ruffling feathers? The description was key.

We settled on the most accurate yet innocuous description, but one with enough catch words to get the right audience: "For sale: organic potato shaped exactly like a cross. Some might call it holy, some might call it biblical. We call it amazing. A conversation piece, at least."

We photographed the potato in flattering natural light and took its measurements. We had to decide on a price, which is not easy considering we were hoping to get at least sixty thousand dollars. Everyone knows that a high starting bid on eBay is the kiss of death, so we settled on five dollars. We just hoped our golden goose would not rot before it sold. A quick glance through a book on root vegetables and we discovered that the potato could last for years if kept in a cool, dry place. We placed the pampered potato in the refrigerator on the highest shelf, between the box of Arm and Hammer Baking Soda and the jar of Patak's Original Extra Hot Curry Paste.

To post our item, we had many options, boldface or plain script, one photo or several, with border or without. Our choices ended up costing us $3.85, which would leave us a net profit of $59,996.15.

We also had to decide on the categories for eBay where our item would be listed, so we went with "Religion" and "Totally Bizarre." I should have looked at the latter before committing to it since I soon discovered that it contains mainly naked pictures of ex-girlfriends. If we could only redirect man's relentless pursuit of naked pictures into an alternative fuel, we would solve so many problems at once.

After we paid the fee, we looked up our item and were shocked to discover that we actually had competition, a potato chip with a cross in it. The seller of that fried root had written, "Leisurely eating a 2¾-oz. bag of chips when one is discovered with a 'perfect' cross in the center of the chip! Empty bag that it came from is included free." The description was accompanied by a photo, albeit a somewhat fuzzy one. There was already one bid, for ninety-nine cents.

My ten-year-old pointed out the obvious flaw. "How do you send a potato chip without breaking it?" she asked.

Our potato had more potential.

We had paid extra for our item to be listed for ten days, instead of the usual seven. We figured more days meant more publicity, which meant higher bids.

Sadly, no one, not one person, bid on our cross-shaped potato. We felt cheated. After pondering why some people make money selling useless things, while others cannot even sell a cross-shaped potato, it dawned on me that this was a blessing in disguise. If we had sold our potato for sixty grand, my children would never have agreed to do their homework again. Why should they trudge through trigonometry when they can make a living fishing for idiots? Why would anyone in his right mind buy a cross-shaped potato? Our failure to find a person stupid enough restored my faith in mankind. Nonetheless, I kept the potato just in case I ever came across an ad reading, "Looking for cross-shaped potato. Will pay big bucks."

But this story has a sad ending. One day, while on a cleaning frenzy, the Frenchman threw out the potato, claiming it had "sprouted." Granted, one year in the refrigerator and that can happen to a root vegetable. Although some might consider throwing out a food item that is growing a stem and leaves "normal," I felt it was an unjustified act of aggression. The children were also upset, not just because they had grown attached to the potato but because now they must find another way to pay for college.

Vink, Vink

I had always sworn that I would never, ever go on a cruise. The idea of masses of random people in an enclosed space rushing to the buffet line has always made me want to strap on a life vest and jump, right there in my living room. I am, however, grateful for people who choose to spend their holidays on those floating behemoths, since all those people will not be vacationing where I go.

Last year, my husband received a travel brochure about private cruises that sail to little-known Greek islands. These idyllic destinations, scattered in the Mediterranean like Easter eggs waiting to be found, evoked such a severe case of wanderlust that I had to sit down on the sofa and stare into space for a considerable amount of time, effectively tuning out the steady chorus of "Mom, what's for dinner?" I was overcome by images of fishing villages with whitewashed houses, hills bursting with fig trees and grapevines, and close-ups of fresh seafood platters that made me swoon. There were also images of the boats used on these cruises, shiny, mahogany-trimmed floating works of art, equipped with professional chefs and staff members who look like Pierce Brosnan . . . Pierce Brosnan *in uniform*.

In my parallel life, the one that takes place entirely in my head, that is the type of cruise I would take. My wardrobe, all off-white linen with nary a wrinkle, would accentuate my fine taste in accessories and my well-toned upper arms. In my parallel life, I am devoted to upper-arm exercises. In fact, I am so devoted that when I travel and don't have access to my dumbbells, I just use cans of diced tomatoes, maize, chayote, or whatever canned vegetable I find. You won't catch me missing a day of triceps and biceps curls just because I'm deep in the jungles of Costa Rica!

And it was with these thoughts that I found myself packing for our cruise—just me, my husband, our two children, 47 of my relatives, and 2,453 random people. The occasion was my father's surprise eightieth birthday. With relatives spanning the age and ability spectrum, our only viable option was a cruise, not the cruise of my armchair travels but one aboard what is basically a floating Nebraska.

I was actually excited to go, not because of the nine restaurants onboard, the karaoke bar, or the tribute to Andrew Lloyd Weber, but because of the opportunity to finally spend seven days with my extended family. We used to spend week-long vacations together regularly in Iran, vacations that allowed me to get to know my aunts and uncles as well as I know my parents. It was during these vacations that I came to realize that "cousin" is another word for "someone better than sibling." These are the ties that have been the secret to our survival as immigrants; it's like a built-in safety net.

In America, we no longer spend vacations with my aunts, uncles, and cousins. Who has time, not to mention the same schedule? We get together for meals, but three hours isn't enough to get to know someone really well; good stories don't happen till the third day anyway. Perhaps this is part of the burden of opportunity, the price we pay for our lifestyles in our new country. Yes, we own a lot of things we never had in Iran—automatic garage door openers, panini presses, and houses with more toilets than most train stations in Asia—but we work and we work and we work. We don't have time for vacations; nor do we have time to use our panini presses.

Our Alaskan cruise would be my father's first-ever birthday celebration. He was turning eighty . . . or so. My father does not have a birth certificate, so he and his siblings have all estimated their birth dates, dates that they all have agreed upon, except for my father. In the past ten years, my father has insisted that he is younger than previously thought. His arguments usually start with "my feet are still very soft," followed by "feel them." Then he goes on to describe all the foods he can eat before bedtime and still get a good night's sleep: "curry, those egg rolls at P.F. Chang's, kabob, *koofteh* . . ." This argument is always followed by a rebuttal by my mother, who insists that in fact, he, like most people above a certain age, does not sleep well when he eats those foods, which is then followed by my father insisting that he does. This goes on until someone announces that dinner is ready, at which time my father rushes to the table, eager to prove my mother wrong.

The first day of the cruise consisted of everyone finding his

room, unpacking, and participating in the mandatory evacu-
ation drill. We were instructed to carry our life vests from our
rooms to the appropriate deck, put on the life vests, then line
up in the designated spot for roll call.

Some of my relatives had a hard time reaching the deck because they had put on their life vests in their cabins, despite
the Please Do Not Put on Life Vest in Your Cabin sign. It had
taken them a while to maneuver their way, like bumper cars,
down the narrow hallways. To the naïve person, this may
seem like a result of the language barrier, but anyone who has
spent time in other parts of the world knows better. Whether
the sign says "Stop," "Do not put your feet on the chair," or,
like the ones barely visible through the haze in restaurants in
France, "Fumer interdit," most people do what they are
going to do. If humans actually followed rules, we would all
be Swiss.

Once we lined up on deck, we were introduced to the ritual of "Smile!" and click. Every single move on the cruise
ship was photographed—then offered for purchase. Who
wouldn't want to spend twenty dollars on a photo of himself
strapped in a bulky orange life vest? Who wouldn't want a
photo of himself holding the dinner menu and leaning toward
his wife, who is also holding the dinner menu? My father, for
one. Throughout the week, he kept interrogating relatives
about the number of photos they had purchased, then con-
verting that to Iranian currency and letting them know what
that money would have purchased in prerevolutionary Iran.
This naturally led to a discussion of how the revolution had
derailed his life, which led to the often-discussed "I wish I had
bought a house in California in 1972."

Fortunately, by this point in my father's speech, it was time
for a meal, which on a cruise is defined as the time when one

is not asleep or in the bathroom. I can only imagine the letters the international staff members write to their relatives in the Philippines, Ukraine, and Romania: "It is amazing the ship has not yet sunk."

Not only did the ship's restaurants present an array of food choices at every meal, but passengers also had the option of receiving, for an extra thirty-five dollars, a large plastic tumbler that enabled the owner, every day, all day, to drink as much soda as he or she wanted. I often saw entire families, each member with his own tumbler, walking around, as if the ship's deck were really the Serengeti and they had not just finished a meal twenty minutes ago. Judging by the obvious man-to-cup bond, I would not want to be the person to tell them, "No, you can't take that with you on the lifeboat."

My father's birthday party was scheduled for the fourth night of the cruise. That night was significant; it was the only night when a table for fifty-one was available. I had the party hats ready, and these had not been easy to find. According to the decision makers in the world of party supplies, people turn "Fifty and Fabulous!" or "Sixty and Sexy!" but then the merriment stops. "Eighty and What Was I Saying?" was nowhere to be found. There was nothing for ninety either. Someone needs to seize this marketing opportunity but quickly.

I ended up purchasing hats that read "30!" With the help of my daughter and a permanent marker, the threes became eights. My relatives each received a conical hat that uniformly evoked the same comment: "I'm not wearing this."

When my father entered the restaurant, we all started singing "Happy Birthday" in English. We wanted to sing in Persian (*tavalod, tavalod, tavalodet mubarak . . .*) but a large group of Middle Easterners these days scares people enough.

Add to that any form of exuberance with clapping, cheering, and guttural sounds and next thing you know, we are trying to convince the nice men from Homeland Security that we are not plotting to take over the buffet lines.

After we finished singing and clapping and cheering, a man who introduced himself as Chuck told my father that it was also his eightieth birthday, but he was not as fortunate to be surrounded by so many family members. My father, wearing his 80! birthday hat, said to Chuck, "It's not my birthday and I'm not eighty."

Usually I try to fix things. I am the interpreter, the cultural bridge, the one who calls the insurance people when they claim that my mom's foot surgery is cosmetic and therefore not covered. But this evening I suppressed the urge to explain anything to Chuck. I watched him walk back to his table and sit down. I wouldn't have known where to begin.

The highlight of the cruise came on the last evening, when after six days of "If we were geese, the foie gras would now be ready," the Midnight Chocolate Buffet was announced. This event was to be held in the back of the ship. I only hoped that by staying in my room in the front of the ship, I would be able to prevent the ship from tilting. I did.

François had decided to go, as he put it, "for anthropological research." I stayed in the room happily rereading *Love in the Time of Cholera*. I waited and waited, but by the time François returned, I was fast asleep. He woke me up, breathless with excitement. This is what a midnight rendezvous with chocolate does to a man. "You should have seen this!" he said, holding a paper plate piled with various shades of brown. "There was an hour-long wait. All your relatives were there, by the way."

"They're your relatives, too," I reminded him.

Apparently, the trash disposals had malfunctioned and the entire back of the ship, next to the chocolate buffet, stank like a day's worth of trash produced by twenty-five hundred people on an enclosed ship. "It was unbearable," he said. "But everyone held their noses and waited. And I can tell you this, it wasn't even good chocolate," he said, taking a bite of the chocolate-marshmallow-caramel-coconut square he'd brought back. "It's like Halloween quality—overly sweet, not very much cocoa, just junk," he added, finishing a chocolate macaroon.

"Floss well," I said.

When we returned from the cruise, bloated with memories, I wrote a magazine article about my father's eightieth birthday party. When the editor sent me the proofs for the piece, an illustration of a conical birthday hat with the saying "Eighty and Flirty!" had been added. I asked the editor to please remove the word "flirty," since I had never used that word. The editor and I e-mailed back and forth a few times, with him telling me it was funny, and me telling him it was insulting. To his credit, he agreed to remove it.

When the article came out, I told my father the story of the undignified illustration and the ensuing e-mails with the editor. "I fought for you," I told him. "Of course I will never get published in that magazine again, but such is the price of dignity. It was worth it."

My dad let my words of courage sink in. Then he asked me what "fe-lare-tee" meant.

I told him.

"But I *like* that," he said.

Peelings, Nothing More
Than Peelings

As the youngest child in my family and the only girl, I was my mother's constant companion. Unlike today's overscheduled children, I had nothing to do all day but wander in my garden or follow my mother. Where she went, I went.

She and I didn't talk much, not for lack of affection but because my mother just wasn't the type to have a lengthy conversation with a five-year-old. Instead, she held my hand firmly as she went about her daily routine, a routine that introduced me to the same cast of characters every week: the vegetable vendor who always offered me a sugar cube with his dirty fingers; the fishmonger, Mashti *seh kaleh* ("three-headed Mashti"), who although possessing only one head, possessed a rather large one; and the butcher with his bloodied apron, who simply scared me.

All the vendors treated my mother with respect, not just

because she was a customer but because of her fair complexion. Our "European" look put my mother and me a couple of rungs higher on the social ladder, but it also meant that my mother, often mistaken for a *farangi,* or foreigner, was often charged more.

When my mother wasn't haggling with the fishmonger over the price of his catch from the River Karun, she could be found haggling over the price of imported Kuwaiti bananas.

Bananas were very expensive in Abadan and happened to be the favorite fruit in the Jazayeri family. My mother could never buy enough.

One day, the postman knocked on our door and handed my mother an enormous box.

"What is this?" my mother asked.

"I just deliver," he responded, waiting for a tip.

My mother gave him a few *toumans.* She closed the door and opened the box. It was bursting with bananas.

My mother, breathless with excitement, called my father at work. "Kazem!" she exclaimed. "Someone sent us a box of bananas. There's no return address. Who could have done this?"

"God works in mysterious ways," my father explained. "I'll be home soon."

My mother hung up the phone and called my aunt Sedigeh.

"*Bavaret nemeesheh!* You won't believe this," my mother exclaimed. "I have bananas for everyone."

"Who are they from?" my aunt asked.

"God," my mother announced.

Ten minutes later, my aunt Sedigeh, my cousins Mohammad, Mehdi, and Mehrdad, my two brothers, Farid and Farshid, our servant Naneh Pooran, my aunt's servant Ali, and my mother sat staring in disbelief at an enormous pile of bananas. With laughter and glee, the mad peeling began. One banana after another was consumed. High on potassium, we delighted in our good fortune.

Before all the bananas disappeared, my mother suggested to my aunt Sedigeh that she should save a few to mail to her son Mahmood, who was studying in Tehran. My aunt Sedigeh tucked a few of the greener ones in her purse.

Half an hour later, the only proof that the banana buffet had not been a dream was the mountain of banana peels that served as a reminder of God's love for us.

Then the doorbell rang. It was the postman.

In a panic, he exclaimed, "I delivered the wrong box to your house. It was meant for the Javaheris, not the Jazayeris."

God does indeed work in mysterious ways, although not as mysteriously as the Iranian postal system.

Unable to hide her shame, my mother apologized. "*Bebakhsheed,* I am so sorry," she said, "but what was in the box is no longer available."

My mother called my father and explained the situation.

"It was an honest mistake," my father said. "No one will ever know."

A few months later, the new school year began. On the first day of school, my brother Farshid wore his new clothes, his new shoes, combed his newly cut hair, and went with my parents to meet his new teacher.

The teacher looked at my parents.

They looked at her.

My parents suddenly wished they were invisible.

Her name was Mrs. Javaheri.

From that day on, on every possible occasion, Farshid presented Mrs. Javaheri with a bouquet of bananas. And Mrs. Javaheri, thankfully, always smiled.

Of Mice and Mandalas

I was staying at my parents' house in Newport Beach when I received an invitation for a speaking gig in Palm Springs. I had never heard of the organization, they would be meeting at six in the morning, and there was no mention of a speaking fee—all bad signs. I thanked them but turned them down.

I made the mistake of mentioning this to my parents. "What?" my father said. "We would have come with you! Remember the Date Festival?"

My parents and I had attended the Date Festival near Palm Springs back in the seventies. Like the Garlic Festival, which we had also attended, the Date Festival was essentially an excuse to walk around eating deep-fried foods on a stick. There had also been, of course, carnival rides I wasn't allowed to go on, thanks to my father, the engineer. "Who assembles these? One loose screw and you're dead. Here, have a funnel cake."

There also had been the requisite pageant, with the local high school girls all dressed up, and the stand with the baby animals, which I wanted to touch but which were also off-limits. "See those children touching the goats? They're all gonna be sick tomorrow and they won't know why. Let's buy some curly fries," my dad offered.

One day after rejecting the speaking gig, I received another e-mail from the same organization letting me know that I should reconsider. "Our members are a powerful and successful group of people, all at the top of their careers. Speaking for us could launch your career in unimaginable ways. Our members do not believe in limits."

I had been a published author for only a few months and had spoken at some bookstores, libraries, senior homes, and book clubs. I knew that it was up to me to spread the word about my book, but I had no way of judging which gigs I should accept and which I should decline. I was afraid that the one I passed up would be the one with Oprah's cousin in the audience. Up to that point, I had said yes to everything, but this Palm Springs invitation was too far and entailed spending the night in a hotel, for which I would have to pay.

I e-mailed back and asked how many people would be attending the meeting and if any of their members were in the media.

I received a cryptic response: "We have hundreds of members, although due to their hectic work schedules, not every member attends every meeting. They represent many creative fields. We cannot, however, divulge the details of their careers. We can only say that they represent the top tier of their chosen fields."

The response, which I shared with my father, left me with

a creepy feeling. My father had a different interpretation: "Very successful people are secretive. We should go."

That is when I remembered the late Bob Hope, Palm Springs' most famous resident. It suddenly dawned on me that many old-time Hollywood people live in Palm Springs, and maybe this was their meeting. Who else would belong to an organization that met at the crack of dawn? Wheeler-dealer Hollywood types who want to play golf afterward and wheel and deal, that's who. These were probably people on the lookout for new talent, the types who, with one push of the speed-dial, could get me on a local but influential cable show hosted by a well-tanned and well-connected insider who would spread the word about me at the tennis club. Next thing I know, I'm telling the personal shopper at Nordstrom that I need a flattering monochromatic outfit for the morning shows.

I accepted the invitation and made a reservation at a hotel in Palm Springs for the following week. My parents, always looking for any excuse to leave their condo, came along.

It had been years since I had shared a room with my parents, and it will be years, if ever, before I do it again. My father, like most men of a certain age, snores. My mother, like most women of a certain age, has insomnia. As I lay on the sofa bed next to my parents' king-size bed, I was forced to listen to my father's rhythmic sonata interrupted periodically by my mother's voice: "Firoozeh, are you awake? I am."

Five o'clock rolled around eventually. We woke up my father, who declared the mattress "one of the most comfortable ever." We all got dressed, grabbed the unused shampoo, conditioner, shower cap, and sewing kit, and checked out of the hotel.

We arrived at the conference center at 5:45 in the morning, just as I had been instructed. There were about sixty people there already, which surprised me, but then again, these people didn't mess around. Our escort—a woman dressed in a conservative suit with a scarf tied in a knot that only French women and flight attendants know how to make—immediately greeted us. She gave us our preprinted name tags and asked us to sign a document agreeing that we would not record the meeting or take any pictures. This was a first for me. She then led us to the breakfast buffet. "Here we have scrambled eggs, Canadian bacon, sausage, smoked ham, ham and cheese croissants, and prosciutto with figs," she said.

"I'm guessing not a lot of Jewish or Muslim members, huh?" I quipped.

"What do you mean?" she asked.

"I'm just kidding," I said, knowing that if I have to say "I'm just kidding," it's a bad sign.

She looked perplexed.

"Not a pig left in Palm Springs," I said, throwing my head back with a fake jolly laugh.

"Excuse me?" she said, looking confused.

"I just said that since there are so many pork products at this breakfast and, traditionally, Muslims and Jews don't eat ham, it would seem that you don't have a lot of Jewish or Muslim members. Of course I could be totally wrong, since many Jews and Muslims eat ham, although most don't, but many do," I said, completely regretting every word I had uttered for the last two minutes.

"Is that a problem for you and your parents?" the woman asked, looking panicked.

"No, no, of course not! We love all things porcine, really," I said, piling my plate as proof.

She then escorted us to our designated table. "I'll be right back," she said. She walked up to one of the members and whispered something in his ear. He looked over at us, visibly alarmed. I took a big bite of the Canadian bacon, made an exaggerated look of satisfaction, and smiled at them both.

At six thirty sharp, the president of the organization took the stage and welcomed everyone. He introduced a couple of new members. "It is now time," he said, pausing for effect, "for joy. Any testimonials?"

Half a dozen hands shot up in the air.

He called on a woman wearing an enormously loud purple and fuchsia caftan.

She stood up. "I just wanted to share with all of you that I just returned from a month at an orphanage in Gwa-tay-mah-lah," she said, pronouncing "Guatemala" with a heavy Spanish accent giving the impression that she had melded with that culture. "During the time I spent down there," she continued, "I introduced the children to the power of visualization. I led workshops every day, and those children," she paused, "were just transformed." At this point, she stopped to wipe her tears. "And they really got it!" she exclaimed. Several people in the room pumped their fists and shouted, "Feel it!"

"Feel it!" she shouted back. "Feel it!"

My mother leaned over. "What did she say?"

"I'll tell you later," I told her.

Next a middle-aged man stood up. "I wanted to let you all know that my instructional CD *Mandala for the Office* is now available. If you want to maximize your potential and change your inner professional landscape, the two-CD set is here for seventy-nine ninety-nine. I've been told by people who have used it that it has transformed their energy field and optimized the level of productivity beyond their wildest dreams. No personal checks, please."

A faint voice from the back of the room sputtered a somewhat hesitant "Feel it!"

"Feel it," Mandala Man responded, sounding none too pleased.

Next a very buff man stood up. He looked like he would be selling either tax shelters in the Bahamas or herbal mixtures to cure whatever ails you. "For all of you interested in exploring Sacred Breath," he said, "I have self-published my book detailing chi energy, bio energy, and of course life energy. This is obviously not for everyone. Most people are afraid of living at their full potential. We use only five percent of our capabilities. That's the comfort zone. If you're not afraid to reach the frontier of maximum output—inner, outer, and in between—this book is for you. I'll be signing copies at the end of the meeting. Cash only, please."

My mom leaned toward me. "What did he say?" she asked.

"I'll tell you later," I said, realizing that I should have passed on this event.

The host announced that there was time for one more. "You," he said, pointing to a young woman sitting behind me.

A somewhat nervous woman stood up. "Um, I just wanted to say that, um, for everyone who had their auras photographed with my Kirlian camera, I'm now making um, customized frames. Thank you." She sat down before anyone could shout anything.

The host then announced that it was time for his favorite part of the meeting, The Topic. "The Topic today," he said, "is overcoming obstacles." Everyone oohed, pondering the depth of his words. "As you know," he continued, "our speaker today is from I-ran. Of course being from I-ran, she has had to overcome a great deal, with the revolution and the hostages and all." Everyone oohed again, perhaps mistaking me for one of the hostages. "Now, you know the drill. First, you tell a little something about yourself, and then you discuss The Topic. You have fifteen minutes."

There were eight people at each table. The woman across from me stood up, introduced herself, and told us that she was a minister in a church that I had never heard of. This very attractive, well-dressed woman told us that as a little girl, she had grown up "on the wrong side of the tracks." She stared right at me when she said this, as if I had been on the same wrong side. "But I found my path, and here I am, helping others find their path." The man next to her hugged her, for a bit too long, I thought.

The woman next to her stood up. "My whole life," she said, "I had been searching for something that I couldn't find until I reached within and overcame my greatest obstacle, fear." Everyone at the table oohed, as if that thought were not already on coffee mugs and bumper stickers everywhere. "Now," she said, "I am a life coach and I walk with others along the same path of self-discovery." No one hugged her.

Then it was my mom's turn. "What am I supposed to do?" she asked me in Persian. There was no time to translate this event for my mom. The Persian language does not have the vocabulary to accommodate these people. We're practical people without mandalas.

"What my mom wants to share with you—" I said.

"Excuse me!" The life coach stood up. "This is a chance for *her* to speak, not *you*."

"I understand," I said, "but my mother's English is not too good."

"I think not!" the woman said, while the minister from the church I had never heard of nodded vehemently. "It's time you let *her* shine. Do not block her!"

This was a woman looking for a cause in all the wrong places. I shut up and looked at my mother.

"Vat I say?" she said.

The life coach held my mother's hands and said, "Tell us what has been hard in your life. What life lessons have you learned during your journey, this journey that has brought you here today?"

"Vat?" my mother said.

My father, who was busy with his second helping of pork products, said, "*Ye harfi bezan.* Just say something."

"Excuse me," the minister said, glaring at my father. "Please give her space to feel. Do not rush her!"

"*Een kholeh.* She's crazy," my father said, in Persian, peeling prosciutto off a fig.

Meanwhile, the life coach finally let go of my mother's hands, realizing they were not a lever for her mouth.

"I come to Amrika," my mother said, and "Eez very good." That was all she had to say.

The life coach and the minister both came to give her a hug. "You are a courageous woman," they said.

My mother felt emboldened. She continued, "And I don't espeak Engeleesh very vell but eez good. I like peepel. Tank you very much."

"Yes," they said. "You speak beautifully! You speak from the heart! Never let anyone speak for you!" Then they both glared at me.

My mother looked pleased with herself. Luckily, she had

taken so long to utter her three sentences that there was no time for the rest of us to speak.

"*Khoda ra shokr.* Thank God," my father said, wiping croissant crumbs off his lap.

The host announced that it was time for the speaker from I-ran. It was the first time I would be speaking at seven in the morning. It was also the first time my speech would be punctuated with audience members yelling, "Feel it!" The first few times, it threw me off, but my inner evangelist caught on quickly. I even asked the audience a couple of times, "Do you feel it?" to which they responded with a resounding "Feel it!" At least they were awake and very responsive, albeit in a grammatically incorrect way.

After my speech, I went to the signing table, next to the lady at the cashier. They had my book there, all three copies. "Excuse me," I said, "where are the rest of the books?"

"That's it, honey," the lady at the cashier said. "We don't sell a lot of books here."

I had made a five-hour round-trip drive, spent $250 on a hotel room, endured a sleepless night, all for the pleasure of selling three copies of my book, maybe.

I sat down between Mandala Man and a woman selling homemade candles in clamshells. A woman approached me. "I loved what you had to say," she said. "Would you like to have your aura photographed? You have a turquoise aura, you know," she told me.

"That's funny because my first name means 'turquoise' in Persian. It's in the book. Would you like a copy?"

"No, thank you," she said.

"I don't want my aura photographed," I told her.

Mandala Man leaned over. "Hey, Foroozi, how 'bout you buy my CD set and I buy one of your books?"

My book could double as a doorstop, whereas his CDs, which cost four times as much as my book, had no use whatsoever.

"I don't have enough cash," I said.

"You can send me a check. You seem really honest," he said.

I wasn't that honest.

"Well, I don't have an office," I said.

"What about your writing space? You can use the mandala for your writing space. Your writing will explode!" he promised.

I imagined words all over the ceiling. "I'll think about it," I said.

"I have only six sets left," he warned me.

The life coach bought a copy of my book for one of her clients. "Can you write in it, 'Hold on tight to those dreams and never, ever let go!'" I did what I was told and even added a waving smiley face, like the one I had learned back in second grade from my crossing guard, Mrs. Popkin. It's funny how we store certain things in our memory bank until just the right moment.

The life coach read what I had written, then pointed to the waving smiley face. "Cute," she said with a snarl.

The minister bought the third and last copy. "I think I'll have your mother sign it," she said.

I was finally free to leave. I stood up and looked for my father, who was easy to find, standing by the coffee urn adding fake hazelnut cream powder to his coffee.

I looked around the room for my mother. There she was, surrounded by an adoring crowd. My mother had morphed into Elvis. I walked over and told her we had to go. Her new circle of friends started hugging her. "You are a nurturing, loving life force," one woman told her. Another told her, "Hold on to who you are." Another told her "to keep reaching."

There was going to be a lot of translating on the drive back.

As we walked back to the car, my father moaned, "Too much salt in that food."

My mother, who after fifty years of marriage, has perfected the art of parallel conversation, said, "Such warm people."

"I don't know why I do this at buffets," my father lamented.

"Yes," my mother said. "I'm glad we came."

Victoria's Hijab

I'm grateful that my twelve-year-old daughter does not have to wear an overcoat and a *hijab*, the headscarf mandatory for all women in present-day Iran. I'm grateful that she can wear whatever she wants and dream of being whatever she wants to be. Her goals have thus far been eclectic. After a class trip to the grocery store in kindergarten, she set as her first career goal to work the conveyor belt that puts plastic wrap on packages of meat. The next class trip to the post office brought forth a new goal. This time she decided she wanted to sort mail—not deliver, but sort. We referred to this as her "zip code" period, distinguished by her constant need to explain zip codes to us and to any and all unsuspecting souls. Her goals continue to evolve. We keep telling her that she will be good at whatever she does, and to make sure that her job comes with health insurance.

Now that she is almost a teenager, I do my best to remain a part of her world. I listen to her favorite songs with her, even though I am not allowed to sing along. This is a particularly hard rule. How can anyone listen to Enrique Iglesias croon "Bailamos" and not sing? I'm singing it now and it's not even playing.

We also read books together. After we read *Marley and Me,* we both cried—she for the dog, me for myself. At least when Marley became arthritic and incontinent he had a loving caretaker. What about me? I explained this to my daughter, who assured me that she would be there for me.

Like any adolescent, my daughter loves clothes, but this is a sensitive topic, not because of her but because of what she is supposed to be wearing according to popular culture. The last time we went shopping I was ready to buy us one-way tickets to the nearest Muslim country. Mind you, I'm no prude. I sunbathe topless in France and celebrate the human body in all its shapes and sizes, but why are the offerings at malls preparing our daughters for careers at Hooters? Why are low-waisted jeans, very short miniskirts, and shirts with bare midriffs available for little girls? I'm all for consumer freedom, but I don't see the freedom when there are no alternatives. What happened to play clothes and girls dreaming of becoming astronauts? I'm not suggesting girls wear bloomers, but didn't there used to be something between Garanimals and thongs? Where did it go?

As we walked into a particular lingerie store, which now carries a line aimed at middle-school and high-school girls, complete with a free stuffed pink dog with every purchase, I took a big breath and did my best to be the open-minded yet boundary-setting mother I aim to be. My daughter had saved her money from her birthday and a stint at chicken-sitting and wanted to buy a pair of sweatpants from this store. Before we entered, I went over the rules: "Nothing written on the butt." (I had lately noticed girls walking around with the word "Juicy" displayed on their derrieres, so I let her know that this was totally unacceptable.) "I know, I know," she said. " 'Not over my dead, decomposing body,' " she added, mimicking me. At least my words had sunk in.

My daughter has a good head on her shoulders. I have never had to do much to set limits beyond just talking to her, but nonetheless, I find that raising a daughter in this culture is a challenge for which no human is fully prepared.

Because I travel, I find myself spending a lot of time in hotel rooms. I do what any fortysomething mom would do: I watch music videos. Inevitably, I am stunned. The first time I saw a hip-hop video, with the cameras pointed up the dancers' skirts while they gyrated, I wondered what their mothers thought of this. People complain about the lyrics in hip-hop, but that's "The Sound of Music" compared to the moves in hip-hop videos. The hills are alive, all right—with perverts. If the point is to sell the music, why must we see the dancers' butts close up and personal? And someone, please tell Christina Aguilera that her stunning voice is enough.

I won't even bother complaining about lyrics. Suffice to say that I miss the days when singers expressed their pangs of love with "Mrs. Brown, you've got a lovely daughter." With today's lyrics, Mrs. Brown would be listening to what exactly the singer wants to do with her daughter, then being asked to join in.

The other popular shows on the music channel involve random groups of college-age students living together, and inevitably hooking up—in every possible permutation. If A has slept with B, and B has slept with C, will A and C be a possible match? It's like Legos but with people. I am often asked why so many people in other countries think Americans have no morals. Well, it's not American spelling bees that are being broadcast around the world. According to what the world is seeing, food is not the only thing that's fast in this country.

Of course it doesn't help that the media is fixated with the bad girls. Should Lindsay Lohan, Paris Hilton, or Britney Spears ever write a memoir—suggested title *I Was Like Totally Wasted*—it could be filled with interchangeable stories of regret, assuming any of them lives long enough to be able to look back on her wasted youth. If they weren't photogenic and rich, would anybody care? There must be unattractive party-till-you-just-can't-party-no-more people out there, but how come we don't see them on the front pages? *That* would be fair and balanced journalism.

Most adults assume that teenagers realize that these girls are not role models, but that's not true. These girls are rich, they're famous, and many girls want to be just like them. In a country where women are told they can be anything they want to be, popular culture tells them that the lower that bar is set, the cooler you are. Having no boundaries and no personal limitations equates to being interesting. The race for the bottom is on. I only wish I didn't have to see so many people's bottoms. There used to be a ditty that children would sing if they saw someone's underwear: "I see England, I see France, I see so and so's underpants." The subject of the song would then be mortified. Those were the days, my friend—and yes, they've ended. Now with the popularity of thongs, we see much more than underwear. It's time to update that ditty: What country rhymes with "cheeks"?

My sister-in-law was raised in Iran and came to America only a few years ago. Throughout her life in Iran, she had to wear a *hijab*. She is one of the most independent, outspoken women I know. She's typical of Iranian women. Wearing the *hijab* does not mean that women are submissive and weak. *Au contraire*. The majority of Iranian women are strong and smart, defying the strict rules set by the totalitarian government every chance they get. I wish to see the day when no woman is forced to wear a *hijab, chador,* or *burqa,* but let us not discount the women underneath those mandatory coverings. If empowerment were as simple as being able to show skin, Paris Hilton would be the most enlightened woman in the United States. Having freedom does not automatically mean we all make good choices. Freedom is a rope: some make a ladder out of it and climb out of the box they're put in; some make a noose; and others make a stripper's pole.

As a mother, I hope my two daughters take their ropes and jump and sing for a really long time. Once their childhoods are over—and not at age eleven, please—I hope they use that rope to climb wherever they wish to go. Then I would want them to hold the rope for others, regardless of what the person is wearing on her head, or not wearing on her bottom.

Pomp It Up

A few years ago, I was asked to deliver a graduation speech at a college. I love speaking at schools, even though most of my invitations are prefaced with, "Khaled Hosseini was not available."

It is a particular honor to be asked to address graduates. Implied is that the speaker has something of value to impart, a bit of wisdom, the right combination of words that will be seared onto fresh, impressionable minds, guiding them throughout their lives like a built-in global positioning system.

I was allotted twenty minutes, which is not a long time for a speech. However, it is an eternity for graduates, who generally have no interest in the speaker and want the ceremony to end so they can drink alcohol. This is most unfortunate, since I know for a fact that many graduation speakers spend weeks thinking of just the right thing to say, then trying to find friends and neighbors willing to listen to three different twenty-minute versions in order to vote for their favorite. But suddenly, it seems that these friends and neighbors have other things to do, even though just minutes before they were hanging out in front of their houses looking aimless.

Before preparing my speech, I reflected upon my high-school and college graduations, trying to remember the nuggets of wisdom passed on to me and reusing them. I could not even remember the speakers, let alone anything they had said. This was a surprisingly liberating thought. Short of tripping on my way to the podium or having a wardrobe malfunction, I was guaranteed to be forgotten.

After much thought and many cups of black tea, I decided to take a cue from David Letterman and make a list of the top ten things graduates should know as they embark upon this thing called Life. I made a point of not using the word "journey," which, given my background in Northern California, showed a lot of self-restraint. It's hard to find a graduation speech these days that does not use the word "journey" at least six times. It is time to retire that analogy and use it only when actual suitcases or Steve Perry are involved.

My father and my cousin Mehrdad had agreed to come to the ceremony, even though they knew no one graduating and the program was three hours long. This is the kind of favor that can be repaid only with a kidney. My mother wanted to come but she was recovering from knee surgery, and three hours seated on metal football bleachers is not good even for the heartiest of souls.

Before beginning my speech, I tried to capture the audience's attention by using language guaranteed to resonate with students. "Listen up," I told them. "There will be a quiz at the end." I distinctly heard one person laughing uproariously. Thank you, Dad.

As I scanned the faces in the audience, I realized that the last time I had been on a football field, I was a member of my high-school drill team. Back then, I was wearing a short pleated skirt and desperately trying to remember the choreographed moves lest I be the one person who made a mistake and got booed. Overcome with relief that such was no longer the case, I realized that for the most part, life only gets better, even if we never look quite as good in short pleated skirts as we did in high school.

Top Ten Things You Should Know

1. There is always room for you to succeed. Many people spend their lives feeling jealous and resentful of the success of others. They believe that life is a pepperoni pizza and every time someone succeeds, one less slice is available. What they don't realize is that this pizza is part of an all-you-can-eat buffet. There's more pizza coming! In fact, the pizza never ends. Don't waste your time and energy thinking about the other guy and why he got his slice before you did. Yours is in the oven.

2. Write thank-you notes. When an interview does not lead to the job—and I guarantee you will experience this many times—write a note thanking the person who took the time to interview you. You will feel like a class act, and the next time there is a job opening, the interviewer will remember you. Paths cross over and over. Assume

you will see the person again. Graciousness leaves a lasting memory; so does "I never wanted this stupid job anyway." I recommend the path of graciousness.

3. Don't get credit cards yet. Credit card companies really,
really want you to have a credit card. Why? Because your
failure is their success! Credit cards are not magic. You
do pay for your purchases. I remember getting my first
credit card after college, with my very own name on it,
and going into Ann Taylor and buying three outfits. It
was like Christmas in July, until I got the bill. I then realized that not only is there no Santa Claus, but there is
something called 18 percent interest, which is like a
whole bunch of evil elves planning to take your money
for nothing. Understand what "interest rate" means. If
you do decide to get a credit card in order to establish
credit, make sure you know how to stick to a budget.
Not knowing how to stick to a limited budget and getting a credit card is like not knowing how to eat sweets
moderately and getting a job in a bakery.

4. Volunteer! Someday scientists will discover that volunteering is nature's Prozac. Until that day, take my word
for it. Whatever you believe in or enjoy doing, there is an
organization that supports it and could use your help.
My freshman year in college, when I was totally miser-
able and the world revolved around me and all my woes,
I volunteered to practice English conversation with foreigners. I was assigned three Korean women whose hus-
bands were studying at UC Berkeley. Every week, these
three women waited for me at the local YWCA, and broke
out in huge smiles as soon as they saw me. They loved
me for no other reason than I devoted sixty minutes of my
week to talking with them. They did not see me through

the same prism I saw myself. They thought I was a winner. I didn't realize it at the time but those women, and those delicious little dumplings they used to bring, were the only things that kept me from total despair. And to think that I had volunteered to help *them*. There's a reason why people get hooked on volunteering. It feels really good and it's not illegal, immoral, or fattening—although I believe the dumplings were.

5. Always have a book to read. Books are like a passport, except they don't just take you to new places. They can take you back in time or forward to an imaginary future or into someone else's head entirely. Books can teach you how to build shelves, catch trout, or cook couscous. They can tell you what life in China was like two thousand years ago. They can make you laugh, cry, think, or just relax. Some books are great for a summer's day at the beach. Ever read a Stephen King novel late at night? Don't. There are so many good books out there! All you have to do is try one. If you don't like it, try another one. Keep going and you will eventually find a book that you enjoy so much that you'll find yourself thinking, "It wouldn't be too bad if I got the flu right now so I could stay in bed and read." Then, when your wonderful book ends, you will be sad. If that book was historical fiction, a graphic novel, or a biography of Babe Ruth, you have found a genre you like. You can look for other books in that category. You are now a richer, more interesting person. I will read a train schedule if that's all there is. I once forgot my reading material on a flight and ended up reading *Sky Mall* out loud to my kids. I even learned something from that. Who knew there's a market for decorative resin gargoyles?

6. Vote! As I speak, there are people languishing in jails around the world. They are guilty of wanting democracy in countries where citizens have no voice. And here, in the United States, we have low voter turnout rates. There is something very, very shameful with that picture. Even if you don't think your vote makes a difference—which it does—vote in honor of those who risk their lives to have the freedom you have. If you don't know how to vote, go to your local library and ask for help. But vote no matter what.

7. Watch less television. When is the last time you heard an accomplished person say, "I owe it all to countless hours of television viewing." Television has become a default activity, a substitute for talking to one another, for exercising, for having a life. I challenge you to turn off your TV for one month. You may miss one or two of your favorite shows but you will survive, and even thrive.

8. You do not have to know, at this very moment, what you want to do with the rest of your life. I did not figure out what I really wanted to do in life until I was thirty-six, but I had worked on and off since I was fourteen. Maybe it won't take you that long. Do your best at every job you have. If your job is to chop onions, be the best onion chopper there is. If your job is to answer the phone, learn how to transfer lines without hanging up on the caller. Keep increasing your skills, through either classes or internships. Stay focused on your next goal. Once you get there, you can refocus and pick another goal. You will eventually end up where you want to be, even if right now you have no idea where that might be.

9. Ladies, if your looks alone open a door, don't go through it. If you get a job because of your appearance rather

than your qualifications, you will pay a higher price for that shortcut than you can imagine. You will get to know the meaning of the word "sleazy." You will also lose your self-respect, and the respect of your co-workers, all of whom will know within days or minutes why you got the job. In other words, it's not worth it.

10. Brush and floss daily. This is an easy one that will save you buckets of money that you can spend on something else, such as a yacht. When it comes to dental care, "prevention" is the magic word. Be one of those people who cannot go to bed without clean teeth. It takes five minutes. If you don't believe me, wait until you get the bill for the complicated dental procedure that awaits you. You will think the dentist made a mistake and added an extra digit. When you inquire about the huge bill, you will find out that, no, he did not make a mistake, and you have to have two more of the same procedure. But don't worry, your dentist will name his yacht after you.

Although I didn't notice anyone taking notes during my speech, I like to think that a few nuggets of wisdom had landed somewhere—perhaps one person flossed vigorously that night. I knew my father was very happy, not just because I spoke but because graduations embody hope and optimism. There were even grandparents among the graduates, all immigrants, who had finally realized their dream of a college diploma. At times like this, I really, really love America.

While I was growing up, my father told me a thousand times that the greatest injustice was his older sister Sedigeh's having to quit school at fourteen to get married. He always said that to deny someone an education is not just a crime but a sin, because you are denying that person the opportunity to realize who he or she is meant to be.

As my father sat on the bleachers with Mehrdad, my aunt Sedigeh's son, I assumed he was thinking about his sister Sedigeh. As the names of the graduates were read, many of them minorities, we all listened. Everything seemed right and full of hope. This was not a fancy college; there was no famous football team, no big-name professors. But these graduates—none of them rich, all with a dream—had accomplished something that will be theirs forever. And although it is too late for my aunt Sedigeh to obtain a college diploma, it wasn't too late for the Vietnamese grandmother who graduated that day. My hat's off to her.

444 Days

I first saw Kathryn Koob on television twenty-eight years ago. I couldn't see what she looked like. Her blindfold covered most of her face. I imagined she must be very scared. My parents and I certainly were. We felt bad about all the hostages, but we felt much worse for the women.

Every day, my family and I watched the news religiously, hoping to hear that the American hostages had been freed from the American embassy in Tehran. My father swore a lot. Whenever the captors were shown, he yelled, "Why are you doing this?" and then he would use some choice words I won't repeat. Whenever Khomeini's bearded, expressionless face was shown, my father yelled, "In which part of the Koran does it say you can take hostages?" Then he'd use some choice words not mentioned in the Koran, either. Even when the news anchors moved on to the next news segment, something inevitably more upbeat, my father kept swearing. He had a lot of time to swear. He was, thanks to the Iranian Revolution, unemployed and, thanks to the hostage situation, unemployable.

We were sure the hostages would be freed by Thanksgiving. They weren't. We hoped they would be freed by Christmas. They weren't. The countdown continued, day one hundred, day two hundred, day three hundred, day four hundred. At the same time, bumper stickers and T-shirts sprouted everywhere telling us Iranians that we were no longer welcome in this country. Of course, that's putting it nicely. It was amazing to me that some people were profiting from the hostage situation by making hateful bumper stickers. What surprised me even more was that there were people willing to buy those bumper stickers and put them on their cars.

I realized something that year. Most people in America watch the evening news to learn about the world, but what they're really seeing is the worst of every country. Only bad news is news. The worse it is, the more coverage it gets. There will never be headline news that says, "Decent Middle Eastern family found! Tune in at eleven for full coverage!"

I imagined what it would be like to come to America knowing nothing about Americans, then watching the evening news for a week. Based on that information alone, no one would leave his house.

Holidays came and went. The two female hostages were shown on both Christmases. One of them was rather witty, which seemed incredible under the circumstances. She made a point of telling her mother not to worry, that her weight loss was intentional. We thought about how hard it must be for the hostages' families. We wondered if seeing their loved ones paraded in front of the camera at Christmas made it harder or easier for their parents and spouses and children. My dad swore some more.

By the time the hostages were finally released, the impression of Iranians as terrorists was firmly embedded in everybody's mind. Forget the Persian king Cyrus, the first ruler ever to issue a declaration of human rights, back in the sixth century B.C., more than a thousand years before the Magna Carta. Forget that King Cyrus is mentioned many times in the Old Testament for freeing the captive Jews from the Babylonians. Forget the contribution of Iranians to literature, music, gardens, and food. Forget that Iranians are famous for their hospitality and that most Americans who have traveled in Iran have loved the country and its people. Four hundred and forty-four days is a long time, seemingly long enough to erase everything good that happened before.

A few years ago, my brother Farshid e-mailed me telling me that one of the former hostages was the aunt of one of his co-workers. I couldn't believe it. I asked for his co-worker's e-mail, and then e-mailed him, asking for an introduction. It was thus that Kathryn Koob, the former hostage who had managed to show her wit and spirit under duress, came back into my life, but this time with eyes wide open and on her own accord.

The first time I e-mailed her, I was not sure if she would respond. I told her that if she wanted nothing to do with Iran and Iranians ever again, I certainly understood. But, I said, I considered myself a bridge builder and would love to get to know her better. I also told her that I wanted to send her a copy of *Funny in Farsi.*

She graciously responded, telling me she has no hatred whatsoever and offered to send me a copy of her book, *Guest of the Revolution.* I devoured her book, which recounted not only the hostage ordeal but her inner struggle to find peace. Her words reminded me of those of Nelson Mandela and Desmond Tutu. I had to meet this former farm girl from Iowa.

Kathryn and I tried to arrange a meeting, but with me in California and her in Iowa, it wasn't so easy. In the fall of 2007, I was invited to speak in her neighboring state of Wisconsin. Kathryn agreed to meet me there.

It was my first visit to the Dairy State, where I learned, among other things, that schools and prisons in Wisconsin are required to serve real butter, not margarine. Should I ever find myself incarcerated, may it be in Wisconsin.

I met Kathryn in the lobby of my hotel. She reminded me of a favorite elementary school teacher or a librarian, someone completely trustworthy who might carry homemade cookies in her purse. Her captors had claimed that all the fifty-two hostages were spies. Kathryn neither looked nor felt like a spy. I'm glad my dad swore at her captors. I only wish they had heard him.

I gave Kathryn my favorite Persian cookbook, knowing that she and Elizabeth Ann Swift, the other female hostage, had cooked for the others. I figured anyone who managed to make donuts while in captivity in the American embassy in Tehran would appreciate a cookbook. During the course of our e-mail correspondence, Kathryn had mentioned her fondness for *khoreshteh fesenjoon,* an exquisite Persian stew made with walnuts and concentrated pomegranate juice. I assumed it would not be easy to find concentrated pomegranate juice in Iowa, so I brought a jar with me. This meant I had to check in my luggage, since any liquid in my carry-on more than three ounces would have been confiscated. That was my contribution to airline safety—no concentrated pomegranate juice on board.

During the course of our e-mail correspondence, Kathryn had asked me if I wanted her to show me her home state of Iowa. I jumped at the chance. Kathryn planned for us to spend one night with her relatives in Albany, Wisconsin, population 1,191, then drive around Iowa.

Kathryn's niece Connie and Connie's husband, Joe, live in a big house with a dog and two cats, a canning kitchen, and an angel collection. The mantel in their family room is covered with photos of multiple generations. Kathryn comes from a family of six, so there were many photos of couples, children, and grandchildren. The crowded mantel, the hostess offering me more homemade dessert, their welcoming a total stranger to their house—all reminded me of my relatives' houses. Of course at my relatives' houses, there are jars of homemade pickled lemons, the people in the mantel photos all look like me, and there's no dog in the house.

We left the next morning at 6:00 AM sharp to drive to Dubuque, where another one of Kathryn's relatives, Gail, was arriving on a steamboat. I discovered that Kathryn has a friend in every port.

Kathryn had gone to Iran in 1979 as the director of the Iran-America Society, a nonprofit organization founded in May 1964 under President Lyndon B. Johnson. The aim of the Iran-America Society, as stated in its charter, was "to foster among Americans and Iranians a greater knowledge of the arts, literature, science, folkways, social customs, economic and political patterns of the United States and Iran, and to develop a deeper understanding of similarities and diversities of the Iranian and American ways of life." Many Iranians, including my brother Farshid, benefited from the excellent English-language classes offered by them.

Prior to her stint in Iran, Kathryn had been stationed in Côte d'Ivoire, Burkina Faso, Niger, Kenya, Romania, and Zambia. I asked her how a farm girl from Iowa ended up traveling all over the world. She told me that she grew up in a houseful of books, courtesy of the Book-of-the-Month Club and the traveling public library. Her mother had been fascinated by China, because it was so far away and unknown. Clearly, a seed had been planted.

Even after the hostage ordeal, Kathryn continued working in the foreign service, with posts in Austria, Germany, and Australia. She still travels extensively.

Once we crossed the Mississippi, we were in Iowa. We met Gail on the steamboat *The American Queen*. Other than the one at Disneyland, this was the only steamboat I had ever seen. We toured the boat, chatted with Kathryn's cousin and her friends, and then headed for Dyersville, where Kathryn wanted to show me the farm toy museum and the Field of Dreams. I had never seen the movie *Field of Dreams*. I have now seen the field.

The farm toy museum was surprisingly interesting and educational. We were the only two people in the entire place, maybe because it was one in the afternoon on a Wednesday. As we walked around looking at the miniature displays, Kathryn told me all about growing up on a farm. The woman knows her farm equipment, including every tool used for harvesting every crop. I will never look at corn or soybeans the same way.

Undoubtedly, Kathryn's practical farm upbringing helped her during her hostage ordeal. She told me that her father used to say, "Yes, life is unfair. What are you going to do about it?" But it was Kathryn's Lutheran faith that allowed her to walk away from the hostage experience without hatred or resentment. She told me that when the Bible says, "Love your enemies," she takes that seriously. Rather than drown in hatred, she tried to see the humanity in her captors. This was not easy. She read the Bible and contemplated its words. "Love your enemies, do good to those who hate you, bless those who curse you, pray for those who mistreat you" (Luke 6:27–28). She realized that in order to find peace, she would have to sacrifice something. After more contemplation, she realized that she would have to sacrifice the anger and resentment.

Not surprisingly—or perhaps surprisingly for some—Kathryn is a firm believer in reconciliation. Having lived in Iran among Iranians, she knows that what she sees on television does not represent the vast majority of Iranians. She knows the real Iran. Almost everyone who advocates war with Iran has never been there. I assume the number one rule in war is "Don't get to know the enemy." Glimpses of shared humanity make it so hard to kill others.

We stopped for sandwiches in a nearby restaurant, splitting a piece of rhubarb crumble pie for dessert. We talked about how rhubarb is used in a stew in Iran. Kathryn told me about all the delicious meals she ate in Iran during the three and a half months she was there before being taken hostage. She told me about receiving a large bouquet of flowers on her birthday from her Iranian colleagues. "You know how lovely those bouquets are in Iran?" she asked me. I was surprised at how well she remembered small details and how much fondness she still carried for the Iran she experienced before her ordeal. She certainly walked the talk. There was not a trace of resentment in her.

After lunch, Kathryn and I drove around. There is a stereotype of Iowa being flat and full of cornfields. That's because Iowa is flat and full of cornfields. Coming from dense California, I found that the open space made me think I was in a different country entirely. Where I live, I'm used to hearing my neighbor's conversations with the gardener, the beeping of the automatic car locks, or basically every word uttered in the summer when the windows are open. Now I know where to go never to hear my neighbors again.

Kathryn decided that I must see the Amish communities in Hazleton and Fairbank. We drove what looked like the same serene roads we had been driving earlier. In fact, every road in Iowa looked like every other road to me—cornfields on one side, a few contented cows on the other, white farmhouses with red barns, and the ubiquitous green John Deere tractor. I'm not good at remembering freeway numbers and always rely on visual memory to find my way. This would not work for me in Iowa.

Seeing the Amish communities was like going back in time—horses and buggies, homes without electricity, and the same, simple clothes worn by everyone. We went into a couple of stores where I bought black walnuts; Kathryn bought a jar of canned beef. I couldn't help but notice that the Amish women have the most beautiful skin. The simplicity and peacefulness of their existence struck me. Their family-centered lives are rich in ways that ours are poor. They have never heard of Lindsay Lohan. They are blessed.

The Amish store sold an array of goods—recipe books, jars of honey and jam, handmade bonnets in all sizes, and galoshes for the men. Horses were tied outside the store, next to our Buick.

On our way to our next destination, driving along a single-lane county road, we saw a group of Amish children returning from school, two by two. The younger kids were skipping and laughing, the older ones, walking and talking; all were swinging their lunch baskets. The girls wore bonnets and modest long-sleeved, ankle-length dresses. The boys wore dark pants and broad-brimmed hats. Against the backdrop of the open fields, this was one of the most beautiful scenes I had ever seen, anywhere.

The Amish do not like to be photographed, so I simply tried to freeze that moment in my mind. I think I will always remember it.

We soon crossed the Wapsipinicon River to Jesup, where Kathryn had grown up. We continued talking, as we had since the moment we first met. On that long stretch of straight road, we suddenly heard a siren. Our adventure would not be complete without a speeding ticket. Kathryn pulled over. As the young officer politely explained that she had exceeded the speed limit, I interrupted. "She was a hostage for four hundred and forty-four days in Iran, and she's showing me around. I'm from Iran." I'm sure that was the first time the officer had heard that excuse, but I suspect he already knew Kathryn. He let us go after Kathryn promised to use cruise control.

We soon reached the town of Waterloo. Forget Napoleon. Forget Abba. Waterloo is John Deere country, where those yellow and green tractors are manufactured. Thanks to my drive through rural Iowa, I now know about tractors, combine harvesters, balers, planters, and seeders. I never thought

I would feel grateful for farming equipment, but having seen the size of those farms in Iowa, I wouldn't want to be plowing those fields by hand.

After showing me the University of Northern Iowa, in Cedar Falls, Kathryn drove us to her home, a charming, well-maintained two-story building with a cross on the front door. Inside, the house was full of books and artifacts from Kathryn's travels to Africa, Europe, and Iran. I particularly admired her figurines and handmade jewelry from Africa, including a lovely bracelet from Zambia. There were many framed pictures of her family and the two sisters from Nepal whom Kathryn had previously hosted and subsequently befriended for years. There were framed embroideries with quotes from the Bible. Kathryn's house was evidence of someone who believes in the Bible but also leaves room for other cultures to believe differently.

The next day, we walked a few blocks to the college where Kathryn teaches. The temperature was in the fifties, or as we say in California, freezing. The students all looked like they were dressed for a spring day. I was the only person bundled in a winter coat, gloves, and a woolen scarf. Perhaps it was obvious where I came from.

Kathryn introduced me to many of her colleagues. She is clearly beloved. Everyone wanted to know if she was available for events, lectures, and courses. It seemed as if everyone needed her for something. I noticed Kathryn rarely said no.

Then it was time to go to the Rotary Club for lunch. My father had been a member of the Rotary Club in Abadan for many years in the 1960s. I have spoken at many Rotary Club meetings so I had an idea of what to expect, but that day, I was taken by surprise. The speaker was a white man from South Africa who had lived in Iowa as an exchange student twenty years earlier. He talked about accepting his responsibility as a white man living and profiting under apartheid. He talked about reconciliation. He talked about his responsibility now as a successful businessman and his goal of improving the lives of his four hundred employees.

The next day, Kathryn took me to the farm south of Jesup, in a community called Jubilee, where she had grown up. Until the end of World War II, Jubilee had a grocery store, a creamery, a blacksmith's, a butcher shop, a post office, and, of course, a church. Today, the only things left of Jubilee are the name, the church, the cemetery, and the memories.

On our way to the airport, I noticed that Kathryn was holding something. She held out her hand. She was holding the bracelet from Zambia that I had admired earlier. "I want you to have this," she said.

For Kathryn, it was the words in the Bible that had helped her endure 444 days of captivity and let go of her justifiable anger. The Bible is foreign to me, but its concepts are not. My father always said that hatred is a waste and never an option. He learned this growing up in Ahwaz, Iran, in a Muslim household. I have tried my best to pass the same message to my children, born and raised in the United States.

Ultimately, it doesn't matter where we learn that lesson. It's just important that we do.

ACKNOWLEDGMENTS

I would like to thank my first agent, Bonnie Nadell, for wanting to work with me when no one else did. Thank you to Mel Berger, Lauren Whitney, and everyone at William Morris for helping me branch out into new areas. It has been my good fortune twice to work with an editor whom I completely trust. Thank you, Bruce Tracy, and everyone at Villard. I hope we have many more projects ahead of us.

A big thank you to Steven Barclay and Sara Bixler, whose talents and competence are both rare and refreshing.

Farshid Jazayeri, Dr. Mahmood Jazayeri, Professor Dr. Mehdi Jazayeri, Ahmad Kiarostami, Professor Abbas Milani, Eli Alfi, and Susanne Pari helped me check my facts about Iran. I thank them for answering all my detailed questions even though they all have other things to do.

I would not have written this book had it not been for the entirely word-of-mouth success of *Funny in Farsi*. If you were one of those mouths, I thank you. To all the teachers and librarians who still believe in the power of books, God bless you! May the idea of shared humanity spread.

Teckie Shackelford, Elizabeth Stahr, Mary Barton, Susan Redfield, Linda Clinard, Carol Jago, Sara Armstrong, Debbie Bloomingdale, Holly Kernan, Sandip Roy, Paymaneh Maghsoudi, Reva Tooley, and Helen Bing have all supported me from the beginning. I thank you.

I could never have reached my speaking engagements had it not been for Kiyomi Masatani and Gary Yamahara, who always accompanied me due to my total lack of sense of direction. They have heard me speak more times than is healthy, and I apologize for any long-term effects they may experience. I am very lucky to have such fine people in my life.

Thank you to Kathryn Koob for her midwestern hospitality.

Were it not for Roberta Immordino taking my baby on three-hour walks, this book would have never been finished. Iolanda Steele packed my belongings and helped me move when my landlady wanted us out the same week I gave birth. Iolanda, you saved my sanity.

And last but not least, to my husband and kids, who make me feel loved all the time, and who are a constant reminder of what is most important in this busy world—I love you. To my extended family, I would not trade you for any other family, not even a Swedish one.

And finally, to you the reader, who still loves a good story, I thank you. If you bought this book at an independent bookstore, I thank you twice.

Laughing Without an Accent

Firoozeh Dumas

A Reader's Guide

A Conversation Between
Firoozeh Dumas and Mark Salzman

Mark Salzman is the author of Iron & Silk, The Laughing Sutra, The Soloist, Lost in Place, Lying Awake, *and* True Notebooks.

Firoozeh first heard of bestselling author Mark Salzman in college, when her husband announced that Mark was one of his favorite contemporary writers. Years later, Firoozeh met Mark at the Sun Valley Writers' Conference and decided that, indeed, the Frenchman was right. Their families soon became friends and, in a strange twist of events, Mark's mother-in-law became Firoozeh's son's fencing instructor. The mother-in-law also regularly gifts the Dumas family with peacock feathers and goose eggs from her yard, but that's a whole other book. Mark's wife, Jessica Yu, is an Oscar-winning filmmaker, and so theirs is the most talented family Firoozeh has ever known. Inexplicably, they are also the nicest.

Mark Salzman: I'm sorry you weren't able to find an eBay buyer for your cross-shaped potato. Just out of curiosity: Is there an equivalent in Muslim culture? Or are Christians unique in placing value on food items that seem to resemble religious icons?

Firoozeh Dumas: It's a new and emerging market in Islam. I am currently looking for members of the squash family that resemble minarets.

MS: You cherish the culture in which you were born, but also appreciate the opportunity to live in this one. You point out that having freedom doesn't automatically mean we all make good choices. Do you think it's possible to have too much freedom?

FD: Our founding fathers assumed the existence of common sense along with freedom, but clearly they never predicted those pants that sag. Every time I visit a high school and walk behind someone displaying three inches of underwear, I think of Benjamin Franklin. But if that's the price we pay for freedom, I'll just have to learn to avert my eyes.

MS: Reading your book made me determined to taste at least some of the foods you described before I die. Could you suggest a sort of Persian Food for Dummies sample menu that I might order from at a restaurant so that I don't order the equivalent of chop suey?

FD: You can always go with the grilled meats—lamb, chicken, or beef. It's just meat, spices, and fire, so it's pretty basic preparation yet full of exotic flavor. For vegetarians, I recommend lentil rice or any eggplant appetizer. Make sure you ask for *tadig,* the crunchy rice on the bottom of the pan. Better yet, try to get invited to the home of an Iranian. We love to feed people while describing our foods. But be forewarned: "No thank you, I'm full" means nothing to us. Wear loose clothing.

MS: Let's play Alternate Universe for a moment. I've just been elected president of the United States and, having read your books, I'm convinced that you would make a tremendously gifted diplomat. I've chosen you to be the U.S. cultural ambassador to Iran. What aspects of American culture would you most like to introduce to contemporary Iranians in hopes of improving their impression of us as a society?

FD: I would begin by assuring Iranians that American teenagers are not like what is shown on MTV and that Pamela Anderson is not a typical American woman. With that hurdle out of the way, I would tell Iranians about the backbone of America, volunteers. I would describe how people in my neighborhood bring food to families in need, even though they have never met. We have a program at my local hospital where trained volunteers hug preemie babies for hours at a time to help them grow. Parents at my local public school make sure that the low-income children never have to pay for school supplies, or yearbooks, or the annual pancake breakfast. A friend of mine, who is rich and could spend all her time getting deep-tissue massages and avocado facials, instead spends her time in a program she started that prepares kids to be the first in their families to go to college. I would also hand out warm chocolate chip cookies at all diplomatic events.

MS: When you first came to this country, you were surprised by how lenient schoolteachers here were compared to school-teachers in Iran. If your school district were to hire you right now as a teacher, how strict do you think you would be?

FD: I have often toyed with the idea of becoming a high school teacher, but I know I would be too strict for this cul-ture. I would want the kids to show respect to me and to one another and I wouldn't put up with any sassiness. I can see myself getting fired already.

MS: In America today, we place a great emphasis on the cul-tivation of our children's self-esteem. Your parents and teach-ers in Iran seemed to assume that your self-esteem would take care of itself as long as you acquired good habits and a suffi-cient degree of knowledge. How on earth did you recover from the damage they must have inflicted upon you by failing to honor your specialness?

FD: Somewhere along the way, the self-esteem movement in America has gone terribly wrong. Self-esteem is not some-thing you can give your kids; we can only give our kids the opportunity to earn it. Self-esteem is not immediate gratifica-tion. Maybe that's why people have resorted to shortcuts. In-stead of encouraging our kids to persevere and do good things so that they can eventually feel good about themselves, we just tell them they're great kids! It's not the same thing.

MS: You are a writer and you are a stay-at-home mom with three children. How do you deal with the challenge of having so little control over your time, especially since you don't have an electronic babysitter (television) in your home?

FD: Every day, there are things that get done, and things that don't get done. I gave up on perfection a long time ago. I am forever indebted to Trader Joe's for having quality frozen foods and vegetables. (This was an unpaid ad, but I am willing to accept compensation, Joe.) Like all moms, I fantasize about having an organized house and toned upper arms, someday. I just do what I can and try to take time to have conversations with each of my kids every day. That's one of my top priorities. I talk with my husband, too, if I'm not too tired.

MS: What is it with immigrants and Costco-style shopping? My wife's grandparents, who were Chinese, would go to Costco and inevitably come home with five cases of relish even though they hardly eat relish. It wasn't really about saving money, because they gave most of the relish away, so it ended up being expensive. Your parents apparently do the same thing. Please explain.

FD: I can't explain. No one is immune. One day I went to Costco to buy paper towels but somehow also wound up with a set of expensive wooden shoehorns for my husband—who has never, ever used a shoehorn—and twelve rolls of wrapping paper. I think there's some KGB-style mind control at work, probably something embedded in the free samples.

MS: Let's imagine that your kids are grown up and have collaborated on a memoir. Please complete this sentence for them: "Our Iranian-American mother tried to be normal, and tried not to embarrass us, but one thing I could never explain to my friends was why she would always . . ."

FD: ". . . engage them in conversation." Apparently, every word I utter to their friends is wrong. Just yesterday I said, "So Tommy, have you made a list of girls you're considering asking to prom this year?" My kids call that embarrassing. I call it making bridges with the younger folk.

MS: To me, you seem completely American (i.e., an "insider"), only with an added dimension—like a computer with an extra hard drive. I feel limited by comparison. But you mention the loneliness of feeling like an outsider here when you were a child and then in college. Do you still feel like an outsider?

FD: Mark, if you're hinting at becoming a dual Iranian/American citizen, I can arrange that. I still feel like an outsider, but now I know that everyone else does, too, so that makes us all insiders. If you read that sentence again, it does make sense.

MS: We in America tend to be puzzled by the tradition of professional mourners, people who feign emotion at funerals. We think: But that's not sincere! Grief ought to be sincere! Can you think of any American customs that, to an Iranian, seem to defy what might be described as emotional logic?

FD: I've always found Thanksgiving to be an interesting holiday. A lot of people absolutely dread having to spend time with their families and yet they have to because of Norman Rockwell. As wonderful a holiday as it can be, it's also a monument to denial: "Let's pretend we get along and then we can avoid each other for another year." I think there should be a sincerity clause embedded in that holiday. If you have to take nine antacids to get through a meal with Uncle Louie and his inappropriate jokes, then you should get a free pass to skip Thanksgiving with the family.

MS: You described a pretty bad day as a parent. Do you have bad days as a writer? Do tell.

FD: I have so little time to write that I generally don't have really, really bad days. I have days when my writing is uninspired and flat. I panic and think that my talent, if I ever had any, has evaporated. But before I can get really morose and angst-ridden, I have to finish the laundry or go to Trader Joe's. (There it is again, Joe. Call me!) So what keeps me from total despair is manual labor in the form of housework. By the way, I am willing to share my housework with any artists who need labor therapy.

MS: You make a good case for the positive benefits of letting go of anger—even justifiable anger—but it's hard to do. How do you manage it? Any tips?

FD: Letting go of justifiable anger is one of the hardest lessons out there. I spent the first few years of my marriage justifiably angry that my husband's family did not like me. Finally, a Catholic friend suggested I talk to a Jesuit priest she knew. I'm a secular Muslim, so it made sense.

The Jesuit priest told me that I would not be able to let anything good into my life until I completely let go of the anger. My father had always said that, too, but sometimes you have to hear something from somebody else for the words to penetrate. I started forcing myself to think of my in-laws simply as flawed humans, just like myself, albeit in a dif-

ferent way. After a while, the anger was replaced with acceptance and even compassion at times.

When my husband and I had children, I never uttered a
bad word to them about their grandparents. I consider that
one of the best decisions I ever made in my life.

My in-laws and I finally had a reunion a few years ago and
my children are getting to know their grandparents. We now
see each other several times a year and our relationship is cor-
dial and nice. We never talk about the past, but we are all trying to make up for lost time. We have also gotten to know my
children's French cousins, who are absolutely delightful.

Thankfully, it no longer takes me years to let go of anger.
Once you learn to let go of anger, you realize what a burden
it is to carry it. Letting go becomes easier with practice.

My Catholic friend, my Muslim father, that Jesuit priest—
they were all on to something!

Questions and Topics for Discussion

1. Firoozeh says that humor differs from one culture to the next, but it also varies from person to person. Is there something that you find hilarious that others don't?

2. In *Laughing Without an Accent,* Firoozeh uses humor to tackle some very difficult topics—like the death of a loved one in "Seyyed Abdullah Jazayeri," or Iranian censorship of her previous book in "Funny in Persian." Do you believe humor is appropriate in all situations? Or are there times when it is not appropriate?

3. Cultural norms are very different from country to country, such as all middle-class families having servants in Iran, unlike in the United States. After reading *Laughing Without an Accent,* which stood out for you? Are there any

from other cultures that you have encountered that surprised you?

4. In "Maid in Iran," we learn that Firoozeh's father changed the life of the maid's son by making sure he had access to education. Do you believe that we each have the power to change the course of someone's life? Why or why not? Who in this culture, besides Oprah, changes lives?

5. In "The Jester and I," a slightly misused word causes a great mix-up. Discuss a time when language barriers or mishaps have caused confusion for you.

6. School is very different in Iran than it is in America. Many Americans believe that the educational system in the United States is failing many of its students. If you agree, what changes would you make? Why is it difficult to make changes? What are the obstacles?

7. In "My Achilles' Meal," we see that Firoozeh's parents felt she was too young to deal with the death of her grandmother. Each culture, and each family, deals with death in a particular way. How does your family deal with death?

8. Firoozeh is guilty of being "the boy who cried wolf" in "Me and Mylanta." Have you ever had a similar experience? Was it difficult to regain the trust of the person involved?

9. Everybody's family embarrasses them. Discuss family quirks that cause you to cringe.

10. It may be true that both kids and adults rely too much on television to entertain them. Do you think not having a tele-

vision would make someone more creative, or unlock some creativity that has been stifled by hours of TV?

11. "In the Closet" proves that Firoozeh's mother definitely believes that one man's trash is another's treasure. Do you believe this is true?

12. Firoozeh writes about the challenges of finding appropriate clothing for her teenage daughter. How do you feel about the clothing choices available for tweens and teens, especially for girls? Do you think the type of clothing one wears affects one's life?

13. Have you ever falsely accused someone of wrongdoing, as in "Doggie Don't"? Did the accusation come back to bite you, as in Firoozeh's case?

14. How would you feel if someone accused you of wrongdoing, or disliked you simply because of where you are from? How does the media's portrayal of people from different countries shape how people feel about them?

15. Firoozeh describes some foods she finds disgusting, whether maggot cheese, bovine urine, or the unsettling *andouillette* described in "Last Mango in Paris." Discuss a time when you were presented with food that you found difficult to eat. How did you react? Was your host offended? Some people travel so that they can try new foods; others do all they can to avoid trying new foods. Which could be said of you?

16. Selling a cross-shaped potato proved not to be the best get-rich-quick scheme for Firoozeh and her son. Have you ever tried a get-rich-quick scheme?

17. If you were to give a graduation speech, what bit of wisdom would you want to impart to the students?

18. Firoozeh made friends with an American once held hostage in Iran. What does this friendship say about the power of the ordinary person to act as a bridge builder? Do you think bridge building between nations is solely the job of politicians?

19. "Most immigrants agree that at some point, we become permanent foreigners, belonging neither here nor there." If you are an immigrant yourself, or the child of an immigrant, do you agree with that statement? If you are not, what could you do to help the immigrants in your community feel at home?

20. What does the term "global citizen" mean to you? Do we have to lose something to become a global citizen, or do we simply gain? Firoozeh was born in Iran and raised in the United States, and is married to a Frenchman. She considers herself a global citizen. But how can others become global citizens? Does it involve living in another culture, or can we simply learn to think globally?

21. Firoozeh says that she thought guilt was a pillar in parenting. Do you know someone who uses guilt effectively? Have you ever used guilt? Did it work?

Originally from Iran, FIROOZEH DUMAS moved with her family to Southern California when she was seven years old. She graduated from the University of California at Berkeley. She lives with her husband and children in Northern California.